CHINESE DIVINATIONS

Other books by Sasha Fenton

Sun Signs
Moon Signs
Rising Signs
The Planets
Understanding Astrology
Reading the Future
Astrology... on the Move!
Your Millennium Forecasts
Astrology for Living
The Moonsign kit (with Jonathan Dee)
Astro-guides: 1995 - 2000 (with Jonathan Dee)
2001 - Your Complete Forecast Guide
(with Jonathan Dee)

Living Palmistry (with Malcolm Wright)
The Book of Palmistry
Fortune-telling by Tarot Cards
Fortune-telling by Tea Leaves
The Aquarian Book of Fortune-telling
The Fortune Teller's Workbook
Tarot in Action!
SuperTarot
The Tarot
Body Reading
Dreams (with Jan Budkowski)
Prophecy for Pro£it (with Jan Budkowski)
Feng Shui for the Home
Star*Date*Oracle ™ (with Jonathan Dee)
Spells

Dedication and thanks
For the family;
including our hamster, Leo.

With grateful thanks to Mr. Li, without whom this book would never have been written, and also to Jonathan Dee for his usual unstinting help and advice.

Quotes
"To understand others is to have knowledge;
To understand oneself is to be illuminated.
To conquer others needs strength;
To conquer oneself is harder still.
To be content with what one has is to be rich.
He that works through violence may get his way;
But only what stays in its place
Can endure.
When one dies one is not lost;
There is no other longevity"
- *Lao Tzu*

"A journey of a thousand miles begins with one step."
– *Mau Tse Tung*

"The journey of a thousand leagues
began with what was under the feet".
- *Lao Tzu*

"These people are undoubtedly cleverer than we are."
- *Henry Kissinger, when secretly negotiating with the Chinese during the Vietnam war.*

About the Author

Sasha Fenton was born in Bushey, near Watford in Hertfordshire, England, and many members of her family have had an interest in psychic or occult subjects. Sasha became interested in palmistry in childhood, partly due to the fact that her mother knew something about it, although Sasha learned her craft initially from books and later by studying people's hands directly.

During her twenties, Sasha read and learned all she could about astrology, and by the time of her Saturn return, around the age of 30, Sasha was earning a little pin money by writing up horoscopes for clients. She soon added Tarot reading to her list of skills.

Sasha is a past Secretary and President of the British Astrological and Psychic Society (BAPS), a past Chairman of the British Advisory Panel on Astrological Education and a past member of the Executive Council of the Writers' Guild of Great Britain.

Together with her husband Jan Budkowski, Sasha started Zambezi Publishing in 1998 and they now plan to publish books written by a variety of skilled practitioners in the mind, body and spirit fields.

Contents

2   Chinese Divinations

ONE

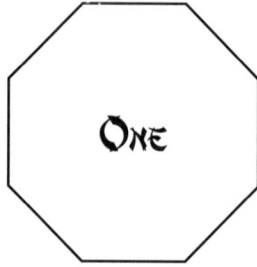

What will This Book Tell You?

This book covers a total of 11 divinations that are in use in China and also in those countries around the Orient where Chinese people have settled.

I have tried to tread a middle way between losing the reader in the mythology, philosophy and complexities of each subject, and of simplifying the text to the extent that the systems lose any relevance or credibility. This book covers as many interesting Chinese systems as I could find. Some are well known, while others are obscure; some are deeply philosophical and others are no more than a bit of fun.

I have used an unusual way of dealing with each subject, which has come out of my experience of teaching mind, body and spirit subjects. Where the more complex subjects such as the I Ching, Lo Shu and astrology are concerned, I avoid the usual step of starting with long-winded introductions or explanations. I start right in by showing ways in which an absolute beginner can use the system on the spot. I then graduate on to more complex uses of the subject, ending with further explanations for those of you who want them.

This enables the reader to get up and running immediately, and then add knowledge gradually as required. I have added a list of further reading at the end of this book for those who become fascinated and decide that they want to know more about any of these subjects.

Links between the divinations

Many of the divinations in this book have common sources and hark back to the systems behind the I Ching or Chinese astrology in one way or another. Face reading and Chinese hand reading borrow some of terminology and concepts from the I Ching. The major divinations of Chinese astrology, the I Ching, the Lo Shu (also known as the Nine Star Ki), the Four Pillars of Destiny and Feng Shui all have cross references from one divination to the next. The oldest root or background to many of the divinations is a very ancient and simplified form of the I Ching, but the Lo Shu is another very ancient form of divination.

Two

A Brief History of Chinese Divination

The Magic Square - The I Ching - Trigrams & Hexagrams

Ancient Chinese legends suggest that the various gods and deities lived in rivers. Many ancient peoples imagined that the gods lived on mountain tops or other inaccessible places, while others saw them as inhabiting the heavens. The Chinese saw rivers as a source of life, both in the form of irrigation and also fish, and of course before trunk roads or railways existed, rivers were the highways that allowed people and goods to traverse great distances.

The Magic Square

Legend has it that Emperor Yu, who lived around 3000 BC, saw a magical tortoise climbing out of a river. He noted the square pattern, along with the lines and colors, on the creature's back and decided that this was to be the basis of the Magic Square. It is this which forms the background to the Lo Shu and Feng Shui. Other sources suggest that the seven stars of the Dipper constellation, in addition to the nearby Pole Star and Vega, form the basis of these divinations and also the earliest forms of Chinese astrology. It is known that that the study of the stars was outlawed at some point in Chinese history, which is why it never developed in the same way as it did in India or in the western world. Despite this proscription, Buddhist monks were allowed to practice the I Ching and the Lo

Shu, and a combination of these techniques eventually developed into the spin-off that we know as Chinese astrology.

An early form of divination involved burning tortoise shells in a fire and reading the resulting cracks that formed when the shells had cooled down. Emperor Fu Hsi was credited with noting down early agricultural and civil engineering ideas, especially those that are connected to rivers. He was also credited with bringing ethics and civilized conduct into the world. His ethical texts were translated into easily remembered verses and some of these became absorbed into the I Ching and other writings.

The I Ching

The most ancient of all the forms of divination seems to be the I Ching. Thousands of years ago, Oriental shamans tried to obtain answers to vexed questions by reading parts of the bodies of animals. After a goat or sheep had been killed for food, its shoulder blade would be roasted over a fire until a crack formed in the drying bone. In these very early divinations, a crack that formed an unbroken line was considered to be Yang, and this would give a positive "yes" answer to a question. A broken Yin line gave a negative "no" answer.

Trigrams & Hexagrams

Once again, it is Emperor Fu Hsi who is credited with turning this original one-line idea into the trigrams of the I Ching. In this case, he seems to have been inspired by the sight of a magical animal called a Hippogriff, which is said to have climbed out of a river and revealed the trigrams of the I Ching along its flanks. The chances are that this animal did actually exist, as even today there are primitive small asses in Mongolia or Siberia, so perhaps one had wandered south after a particularly bad winter. From that time onwards, the I Ching used the three lines of the trigrams rather than the single lines as displayed in the burnt offerings.

The verses of the I Ching were passed down by one generation of scholars after another, until the 17th century BC, when they were noted down on strips of bamboo. In the 12th century BC, King Wen wrote the first commentaries on the trigrams of the I Ching. King Wen then fell foul of Emperor Chou Hsin, but his son, the Duke of Chou, released King Wen and restored him to his throne. Over time, King Wen, his son Tan and the Duke of Chou continued to work on the I Ching, and it is the Duke who is credited with setting two trigrams atop one another to make a hexagram. In the 6th century BC, Confucius and Lao Tze became interested in the system and Confucius wrote further commentaries; it was he who gave the system its name, "I Ching". This name meant something like "intelligent scrolls that show how to deal with events and calamities", but it has became known in the west as the "Book of Changes".

After this period, many philosophies proliferated and different versions and interpretations of the I Ching abounded. Much later, the Emperor Chin unified China once again and gave it strong government. One method that he used to keep control of his subjects was to outlaw writing and scholarly knowledge, including the works of Confucius. Emperor Chin is not the only one to have outlawed books, religion or philosophy, because medieval Christians practiced censorship, while in our own century Hitler, Stalin, the Khmer Rouge and Mao Tse Tung have all banned and destroyed books.

Whether the I Ching was on the list of forbidden knowledge or not, it survived and was passed on orally by the Gypsies who had the advantage of never settling anywhere long enough to be controlled by any government. During the last imperial dynasty, which lasted from 1644 to 1912, the original roots of the I Ching were once again discovered and studied - and this time they remained in print. The Chinese communists disapproved of Chinese divinations, considering them to be useless superstition, but they realized that it was too late to ban them altogether. Chinese divinations have now become so universally known that even if a future government banned them, they would continue to exist in many places outside China - even in books like this one.

THREE

The Ming Shu - Chinese astrology

Working out a Chinese Horoscope - Yang & Yin signs - animals & elements - year dates - animal sign characteristics - the elements & element years - active & receptive - seasons & months - hour signs - Chinese New Year - stems & branches

Many people are put off Chinese astrology because they think that it begins and ends with the year sign, and I am frequently asked how a system that covers a whole year of birthdays can have any relevance. As with any other form of astrology, there are two levels of operation, and the moment one leaves the basics behind and gets into the complexities, a bit of brain-power needs to be applied. I have organized this section in such a way that you can look up the basics, such as Yang and Yin, the animal year sign and the elements, but I have included extra information towards the end of this section of the book for those who want more.

How to work out a Chinese horoscope

1.   If you only want the most basic information, look up your year sign. Take note of whether you belong to an active Yang sign or a receptive Yin sign. Then read the section on the elements for each Chinese animal year sign to discover more about the characteristics for those born during your year.
2.   Check out the larger section on the elements, as this is easy to do and it will add greatly to your knowledge.

3.   If you want to discover the breakdown of the seasons, months and a truly wonderful way of discovering the right Chinese hour for your birth, read this section.

4.   If you like the technical stuff and some explanatory information, read right through to the end of the chapter.

Yang and Yin

Much Chinese philosophical thought depends upon the idea of balance between the active, masculine Yang force and the more passive, feminine Yin force. Without Yang people in the world, there would be no progress, no new enterprises and nobody to fight necessary battles. Without Yin people, the daily chores would never be done, farms and businesses would be neglected, children would come to harm and there would be no continuation.

Every sign is considered to be Yang or Yin in character. Yang signs are assertive, active, courageous and extrovert. When under pressure, Yang people can be offensive and they may bully those who are in no position to stand up to them. Yin people are patient, adaptable, subtle and able to endure, but when under pressure they may whine, behave childishly and become depressed. As you will soon see, the Yang and Yin factor has a very important effect on the character of the elements, which are either Active when under a Yang influence or Receptive when under a Yin influence.

The elements are considered to be neutral, they have no Yang or Yin personalities of their own, so that they can be Yang or Yin depending upon which animal sign is "in office" during any particular year.

Yang and Yin signs

Rat	Active	(Yang)
Ox	Receptive	(Yin)
Tiger	Active	(Yang)
Rabbit	Receptive	(Yin)
Dragon	Active	(Yang)
Snake	Receptive	(Yin)

Horse	Active	(Yang)
Goat	Receptive	(Yin)
Monkey	Active	(Yang)
Rooster	Receptive	(Yin)
Dog	Active	(Yang)
Pig	Receptive	(Yin)

The animals and the elements

The animal signs change every year, but the elements change every two years, and these two-year blocks are sometimes referred to as binomials, which simply means using the same name twice.

Each two year block is assigned to one of five elements, so that although the animal signs repeat every 12 years, they are modified by a different element each time around, until after 60 years the cycle begins again. When the 60-year cycle is complete, each animal will have been through all five elements.

The animal names did not exist in Chinese astrology until Buddhism became popular. Before this, the annual signs were referred to as earthly branches, while the elements were referred to as heavenly stems.

Calling all Aquarians

Those of you who were born at the start of a Chinese New Year under our western sign of Aquarius, are advised to read the sign which precedes as well as the one for your date of birth. You may find that you are more like the sign that has just passed than the one that is coming in, or that you are a mixture of both.

I have commented in more depth on this problem in the technical section at the end of the Chinese astrology section of this book.

The Chinese Astrology Year Dates

Year	Date	Animal Sign	Element
1930	Jan 29	Horse	Active Metal
1931	Feb 17	Goat	Receptive Metal
1932	Feb 6	Monkey	Active Water
1933	Jan 25	Rooster	Receptive Water
1934	Feb 14	Dog	Active Wood
1935	Feb 3	Pig	Receptive Wood
1936	Jan 24	Rat	Active Fire
1937	Feb 11	Ox	Receptive Fire
1938	Jan 31	Tiger	Active Earth
1939	Feb 19	Rabbit	Receptive Earth
1940	Feb 8	Dragon	Active Metal
1941	Jan 27	Snake	Receptive Metal
1942	Feb 15	Horse	Active Water
1943	Feb 4	Goat	Receptive Water
1944	Jan 25	Monkey	Active Wood
1945	Feb 12	Rooster	Receptive Wood
1946	Feb 2	Dog	Active Fire
1947	Jan 22	Pig	Receptive Fire
1948	Feb 10	Rat	Active Earth
1949	Jan 29	Ox	Receptive Earth
1950	Feb 16	Tiger	Active Metal
1951	Feb 6	Rabbit	Receptive Metal
1952	Jan 26	Dragon	Active Water
1953	Feb 14	Snake	Receptive Water
1954	Feb 3	Horse	Active Wood
1955	Jan 24	Goat	Receptive Wood
1956	Feb 11	Monkey	Active Fire
1957	Jan 30	Rooster	Receptive Fire
1958	Feb 18	Dog	Active Earth
1959	Feb 7	Pig	Receptive Earth
1960	Jan 28	Rat	Active Metal
1961	Feb 15	Ox	Receptive Metal

1962	Feb 5	Tiger	Active Water
1963	Jan 25	Rabbit	Receptive Water
1964	Feb 13	Dragon	Active Wood
1965	Feb 1	Snake	Receptive Wood
1966	Jan 21	Horse	Active Fire
1967	Feb 9	Goat	Receptive Fire
1968	Jan 29	Monkey	Active Earth
1969	Feb 16	Rooster	Receptive Earth
1970	Feb 6	Dog	Active Metal
1971	Jan 26	Pig	Receptive Metal
1972	Feb 15	Rat	Active Water
1973	Feb 3	Ox	Receptive Water
1974	Jan 24	Tiger	Active Wood
1975	Feb 11	Rabbit	Receptive Wood
1976	Jan 31	Dragon	Active Fire
1977	Feb 18	Snake	Receptive Fire
1978	Feb 7	Horse	Active Earth
1979	Jan 28	Goat	Receptive Earth
1980	Feb 16	Monkey	Active Metal
1981	Feb 5	Rooster	Receptive Metal
1982	Jan 25	Dog	Active Water
1983	Feb 13	Pig	Receptive Water
1984	Feb 2	Rat	Active Wood
1985	Feb 20	Ox	Receptive Wood
1986	Feb 9	Tiger	Active Fire
1987	Jan 29	Rabbit	Receptive Fire
1988	Feb 17	Dragon	Active Earth
1989	Feb 6	Snake	Receptive Earth
1990	Jan 26	Horse	Active Metal
1991	Feb 14	Goat	Receptive Metal
1992	Feb 3	Monkey	Active Water
1993	Jan 22	Rooster	Receptive Water
1994	Feb 10	Dog	Active Wood
1995	Jan 31	Pig	Receptive Wood
1996	Feb 19	Rat	Active Fire

1997	Feb 7	Ox	Receptive Fire
1998	Jan 28	Tiger	Active Earth
1999	Jan 16	Rabbit	Receptive Earth
2000	Feb 5	Dragon	Active Metal
2001	Jan 24	Snake	Receptive Metal
2002	Feb 12	Horse	Active Water
2003	Feb 1	Goat	Receptive Water
2004	Jan 22	Monkey	Active Wood
2005	Feb 9	Rooster	Receptive Wood
2006	Jan 29	Dog	Active Fire
2007	Feb 18	Pig	Receptive Fire
2008	Feb 7	Rat	Active Earth

The character of each Chinese animal sign

The Rat
Yang

These assertive, intelligent people have a great desire to reach the top. They don't give up easily, they keep their goals in sight even if this means riding roughshod over other people or making use of them. They don't set out to hurt or to upset others, it is simply that they are impatient and they can't help considering their own needs to be paramount, but their charm and humor ensures that they are usually forgiven. The determination of this sign means that it can reach apparently unobtainable goals and keep going in times of adversity. Rats don't have a great air of authority about them and they may not look much like winners, but they succeed even when faced with appalling odds, which invites a mixture of respect, amazement and envy.

Rats have good taste, an artistic eye and they often look very good. Their gossipy sociability and confident exterior hide a complex nature, because they are afraid of failure and they hate to look foolish. Rats hate being rushed into anything or being made to reveal their desires openly. They are not easily influenced, preferring to make up their own minds and to make their own decisions. When pressed by others, they will tell lies in preference to revealing their plans or allowing their vulnerability to show. They succeed in business, the art world, advertising, sales, politics and journalism. Two of the most marked aspects of Rats are their intellect and their academic studiousness. Many Rats study some subject in great depth, and most appear to be deeply interested in psychology and philosophy. On the other hand, Rats are also extremely materialistic, they need a high income and they know how to spend money on things that look good or those things that enhance their image.

These creative types cannot abide an uncomfortable or dirty environment, petty mean-spirited people or those who nag. For those of you who seek a generous, amusing and ambitious partner, you need look no further than the nearest Rat. However, you need money and status, or Rats won't want to be bothered with you.

Rats are compatible with Dragons, who are powerful and self-willed enough not to be deceived by their artfulness, or Monkeys, who are tricky enough to cope with them.

(Remember that the Chinese years do not correspond exactly to the Western calendar. First look up your animal sign in the table at the beginning of this chapter).

Wood Rat (1924,1984)
Ambitious, likeable, farsighted, these Rats tune into upcoming trends. Good talkers. A tough childhood, possibly due to the loss of the parents, thus needing emotional and financial security, and they may worry too much about these things. A caring, romantic and artistic Rat who prefers to live in the country. Works best at night.

Fire Rat (1936, 1996)
Chivalrous, dynamic, idealistic, ambitious, generous, independent. May campaign for causes and fight for justice. Little self-discipline, they lack diplomacy and they can be touchy. Witty but prone to anxiety and overexcitement.

Earth Rat (1948, 2008)

Realistic, thorough, hard working, they slowly climb the ladder of success. Not gamblers. Happy if they marry and create a family later in life when they have achieved some financial stability. Self-righteous and intolerant. Too practical, lacking imagination, stingy. Early marriages are unstable and they find it hard to get along with their offspring. Conservative but generous, practical and able to turn ideas into reality.

Metal Rat (1900, 1960)

Idealistic, deeply emotional, clever with money and investments, athletic. Can put on airs and graces and show off, they suffer from jealousy and envy. Competitive and ruthlessly ambitious, can be money minded or calculating in love relationships.

Water Rat (1912, 1972)

After a difficult childhood, ambition and talent take these Rats far. Intellectual, inspiring respect, shrewd but also diplomatic. Outspoken, over-ambitious, unfeeling and critical at times, but happy with a strong partner. Water Rats like travelling.

The Ox
Yin

Oxen are comfort lovers who are also materialistic and home-loving. Their steady, trustworthy nature makes them reliable, stoical and practical. They take things in their stride and seldom become irritable, although their slow-burn nature can erupt into terrible anger. They are generous to those whom they love, and they hate to take advantage of anyone. Oxen love good food, music and pleasant surroundings, although they prefer family life to the high-life. They are pleasant and charming. They get on well with the opposite sex and - being sensual - they make good lovers.

Oxen are money-minded; they fear loss, poverty or discomfort, and can become greedy and over-materialistic as a result. Oxen can succeed in the arts or in business, but they need financial security, so they rarely enter extremely speculative ventures. Oxen need security in relationships, so they make faithful if rather unimaginative partners. They are physically strong and clever with their hands. As long as they are secure, appreciated and never rushed, they can be very good to live with, or to work with in a business partnership. Oxen are compatible with the Snake and the Rooster.

(Remember that the Chinese years do not correspond exactly to the Western calendar. First look up your animal sign in the table at the beginning of this chapter).

Wood Ox (1925, 1985)
Honest, considerate, sociable, respected for their integrity and ethics, innovative, progressive, ambitious and able to work alone. Can reach heights of wealth and fame. May come from single parent family or poor background, but they make good in later life. Good to their own children later on.

Fire Ox (1937, 1997)
Hard working, honest, fair, happy with a reasonable income, easygoing, drawn to show business and a touch of fame. May be too fond of power, over-ambitious, proud, forceful, materialistic, superiority complex. Easily aroused by love or sex.

Earth Ox (1949,2009)
Practical, hard working, sensible, honest, truthful, self-sufficient, persevering, sincere and loyal to those they love, determined, thorough, uncomplaining. Good business sense. Can be thoughtless, insensitive, outspoken, unimaginative, money-minded or depressive. Both sexes tend to marry twice, and the second marriage is better than the first. Stubborn.

Metal Ox (1901, 1961)
Strong willed, tough, much stamina, determination and drive. Metal Oxen overcome early upheavals in life and they experience many early changes of location and fortune. Some can buck the trend and be quite gentle and kind. Clashes

with others arise because they want their own way. Can be arrogant, narrow minded, unaffectionate and possessive.

Water Ox (1913,1973)

Water Oxen grow up in households where there is material comfort but emotional turmoil. Realistic, calm, patient, determined, reasonable. They work well with others. Refined, practical, clever and successful. Love nature. Can be suspicious and jealous when in love.

The Tiger
Yang

Tigers are great fun. Their sparkling personalities, humor and charm make them fascinating, and they enjoy the company of others. Tigers have a strong sense of justice; they often take the part of the underdog because they hate to see anyone suffer. Their kind hearts and joyful temperaments hide strength and ambition, and because they aim high, they usually get where they want to be. Tigers are excellent bosses but they are far too self-motivated, creative and rebellious to work for others for long. They love to be in charge, using their organizational skills to persuade others to do the dirty work for them. They can find original ways around problems but they would rather not be bothered with trifling details. They rarely forget those who do them a good turn but they never forget a hurt, and once they lose their faith in someone it can never be reinstated.

Tigers work hard and play hard. Their ambition, coupled with their expensive tastes, ensure that they are high earners. They are great company but they can be temperamental to live with. Their nerves are surprisingly easily frayed and they can become overworked and overtired. Tigers need to be in the center of things, gathering up the admiration that they consider to be their due.

Tigers are compatible with Horses and Dogs.

(Remember that the Chinese years do not correspond exactly to the Western calendar. First look up your animal sign in the table at the beginning of this chapter).

Wood Tiger (1914, 1974)

Good negotiators who take charge in a pleasant way. Sociable, charming, innovative. They like to be around celebrities, but while superficially friendly, they may choose to live alone. Wood Tigers gain a comfortable lifestyle. Parents may cause problems, and estrangement can occur. Very romantic and passionate. Could be artistic.

Fire Tiger (1926,1986)

Theatrical, active, adventurous, demonstrative, easily bored, optimistic but also moody. They like to be close to celebrities. Very educated and knowledgeable, clever. Can be schemers who dislike advice or criticism. Women are especially charming and successful. Passionate in love.

Earth Tiger (1938, 1998)

Intelligent, hard working, educated, ambitious, clear headed. They need to get going early in order to make a success of their lives. They also need to leave home and find the right area and the right niche for themselves. Good leaders with sound judgement. Can be jealous and possessive but also loyal and loving.

Metal Tiger (1950, 2010)

Passionate, emotional, glamorous, sometimes very successful, courageous, humorous, committed, born orators, lucky with money. Success is important to the Metal Tiger. Hyperactive, possibly unstable, passionate, aggressive, outspoken, anxious, never satisfied, bad tempered, egotistic, risk-takers. They can be domineering or lacking in understanding. Can become very depressed. Wasteful when young but more sensible later.

Water Tiger (1902, 1962)

Quite shrewd and intuitive. Water Tigers can do well in business, and are ambitious, persuasive. Sincere, generous, humorous, open and honest. Can get into difficulties through leaving things unsettled. Too restless for good relationships, but if marriage and children come later when life is more settled, this can work out well.

The Rabbit

Yin

Refined and tasteful, these people have an air of exclusivity about them; they hold back from others and prefer not to become involved with or excited by anything that doesn't immediately affect their own well-being. People seek out Rabbits for their wise and objective counsel. Rabbits do have feelings, of course, and they can become extremely depressed when hurt, and they find it difficult to wear their hearts on their sleeves. They put a great deal into personal relationships and they take them very seriously. They make excellent working colleagues as long as there is mutual respect.

With their pent-up emotions and sensitive nature, Rabbits can lash out angrily or become coldly sarcastic in an attempt to cover up hurt feelings. Conservative, fascinating and rather difficult to know, Rabbits are admired or disliked but never ignored. They have a certain sexual charisma that results from their reserved attitude, and this, along with their fine minds and fascinating looks, makes them attractive and intriguing.

However detached and self-assured they appear to be, Rabbits hide a strong sense of inadequacy and they strive hard to reach the high standards that they set themselves. Rational, logical and humanitarian, they make wonderful counselors, doctors, teachers and personnel officers. They can cope with the complexity of computers, astrology and philosophic or academic studies. Rabbits are intuitive and they are often attracted to occult or psychic subjects.

They are compatible with Goats and Pigs.

(Remember that the Chinese years do not correspond exactly to the Western calendar. First look up your animal sign in the table at the beginning of this chapter).

Wood Rabbit (1915, 1975)
Intelligent, compassionate, hardworking. These Rabbits enjoy working as part of a team and living a successful if rather ordinary life. Can be excellent athletes or writers. They fit in and rarely rebel. Good with children or when helping the underdog.

Fire Rabbit (1927, 1987)
Popular, fun-loving, good family types. Emotional and a bit eccentric but rarely over-the-top. Full of great ideas, but they may not complete what they begin. Intuitive, possibly a bit psychic, they excel in healing and medical work. May marry twice.

Earth Rabbit (1939, 1999)
Rather ordinary folk who enjoy family life. Not especially ambitious, fairly easygoing, rational, sensible. Best when they marry older or tougher personalities. Can be money-minded, but perhaps only cautious. They need security in marriage.

Metal Rabbit (1951, 2011)
Logical, intelligent, hard working, ambitious, hard to influence, connoisseurs or collectors who need privacy and their own space, and they can be moody. Self-motivated, not dependent upon family. They make good contacts and do well. Protective of others, very caring and defensive of those who need help. May take risks or overestimate abilities. Possessive in love.

Water Rabbit (1903, 1963)
Sensitive souls, emotional and easily upset. Travelers who can cope with unstable finances and lifestyle. They settle for what they have and don't strive for more. They love to eat and drink. Artistic dreamers. Romantic and caring when in love.

The Dragon
Yang

This lucky sign promises health, wealth and happiness. These lively people seem to succeed at whatever they do. Their inventive, intelligent minds lead them to explore widely and to want to experience all that life has to offer. Their strong will, determination, restless independence and need for personal freedom make Dragons unpredictable at times. They follow their own path, even if it seems to be illogical to others. Dragons cannot be made to work in a strict routine because they are easily bored. Dragons are quick tempered and blunt but they rarely set out to hurt, it's just that their honesty seems to get the better of them. They are so amusing and genuinely kind that no one can be angry with them for long. In personal relationships they can be unreliable, because their hatred of routine and their need for exploration can make them unfaithful from time to time, although this is not designed to hurt their partners.

Dragons have high standards, they work hard and they are discriminating and honest. Highly intuitive and extremely interested in philosophical subjects, they may be intellectually drawn to the world of the occult. Good looking with attractive personalities, they don't really understand jealousy - although they can be the cause of it in others. Dragons will succeed in any form of work that pushes back horizons and that allows them to deal with people. Teaching is their specialty, as is salesmanship, politics, advertising and the arts.

Dragons are compatible with Monkeys and Rats.

(Remember that the Chinese years do not correspond exactly to the Western calendar. First look up your animal sign in the table at the beginning of this chapter).

Wood Dragon (1904, 1964)

Logical, intellectual, inventive, admired by others. Independent, so much so that they may choose to live alone. They live quite well, with a comfortable and reasonably happy family life and a happy old age. Can be creative or artistic. Great vision, but may lack practicality. Wonderful lovers.

Fire Dragon (1916, 1976)
Competitive, determined, fighters for causes, or perhaps just for what they want for themselves. These Dragons live full lives and they can be charming, sociable and great fun when they are in the right mood. Lively, adventurous, stimulating. Can have accidents due to rashness.

Earth Dragon (1928, 1988)
Executive ability, outstanding personalities, dogmatic and dictatorial. These Dragons move in the highest circles, they make a success of life and they can become extremely rich. They may marry for money or status, but they can fall out with partners and offspring, and lose touch with them. If these Dragon marry for love, it will work.

Metal Dragon (1940, 2000)
Very strong personalities. Blunt, ambitious, impatient but often also charming. They prefer living the good life with plenty of status and material goodies. Women can be tight-fisted, probably because they hate the thought of poverty. The men are more openhanded. Jealous when in love.

Water Dragon (1952, 2012)
Intelligent and faithful, these Dragons can work too hard, particularly if they come from an impoverished background. They don't take much notice of the opinions of others. Both sexes can do well and become wealthy later in life if they don't take unnecessary risks. Women are inclined to gain weight. They love psychic matters, astrology and the like, and they may dabble in spiritualism and magic. These Dragons love to read. They seek a soul mate for marriage.

The Snake
Yin
Snakes are reserved people whose power is hidden and contained. They are attractive and graceful but not particularly sociable. Snakes are intensely loyal to those they care about and they are totally responsible towards those they employ. They remember good

deeds but they never forget a hurt, and they can wait for years to get their own back. Snakes are hard and reliable workers, perfectionists who are often clever with their hands. These people are ambitious and they can be critical of themselves and of others. They are tenacious and usually committed to finishing everything that they start. Snakes are secretive and nobody really knows how much (or how little) money they have; the state of their emotions is even more sacrosanct than the contents of their bank account. They can come into money as a result of divorce, legacies or sheer luck.

Snakes have an exceptional ability to study and concentrate. Their approach is slow and thorough, but they can cope with fine details. Some Snakes hate small talk and useless socializing, while others love nothing better than a well cooked and presented meal and fine wine in the company of special friends or well-loved relatives. Snakes make excellent inventors, doctors, scientists, engineers, writers and computer buffs. Some are well adapted to dealing with people, while others prefer to wrestle with practical or intellectual problems.

Snakes can switch off from the demands of others, they don't seek approval and they are happy to allow others to think what they like. The Snake's greatest fear is of becoming dependent or of appearing weak or incompetent - even to themselves. Snakes are compatible with Roosters and Oxen.

(Remember that the Chinese years do not correspond exactly to the Western calendar. First look up your animal sign in the table at the beginning of this chapter).

Wood Snake (1905, 1965)

These Snakes may suffer illness, deprivation or hardships during youth, which makes them security conscious. Pleasant and interesting, interested in history. Can't put up with chaos or crowds. They can be vain and fussy about their hair. Sometimes mysterious and keen on intrigue. Can be callous heartbreakers.

Fire Snake (1917, 1977)
Strong, stubborn personalities who can dominate others. Opinionated and critical, these Snakes are self-reliant and self-centered. They look good and they move in the right circles. Ambitious, successful, passionate and possessive, later isolated due to their difficult natures. Expensive tastes, but also refined. Can be "power behind the throne" types. Secretive and self-protective when in love.

Earth Snake (1929, 1989)
Conservative, hard working, clever, balanced, lucky. Fond of order and precision. Good relationships, prosperity, success, happiness and clever property dealings ensure a wonderful life. Can appear unfeeling in relationships.

Metal Snake (1941, 2001)
Difficult personalities who rarely reveal their true goals. Highly ambitious, and successful as long as they avoid alienating those who can help them. Cautious and determined. Tough enemies. Can chop and change careers while seeking the right opportunity. Men marry very young women; women marry older men but both need an intellectual partner.

Water Snake (1953, 2013)
Astute and intelligent, these Snakes go far. They can work their way into the corridors of power. Creative and practical, smart and lucky. They do well in the long run. The intellect is stronger than the feelings, so a career in maths, science or the law may attract. Fastidious and finicky. Need an intellectual lover.

The Horse
Yang
Horses have immense charm; they are attractive, humorous, kindly people who make good friends and excellent work-mates. They work hard, take responsibility and look after their families. Being good looking, charismatic and intelligent, they appeal to the opposite sex. At work, their organizational abilities and capacity for

putting in long hours without tiring ensures success and the respect of others. Horses make good company directors, teachers, lawyers and farmers. Being clever with their hands, they also make good mechanics, dress-designers and builders. Horse people are restless and energetic and they love to travel, and many work as a travelling salespersons. They love interesting holidays and tourist attractions. Horses are popular and cheerful, but they have short tempers and sometimes they will cut off their noses to spite their faces. They can be impulsive and they like having their own way. They are sometimes incredibly self-absorbed and self-centered.

Horses like to think for themselves and they are very independent. If they don't have enough to occupy themselves with, they are easily bored. Their tempers are prodigious and they can lose control if driven too hard, while a tendency for sarcastic outbursts and cold sulky behavior can alienate people. Some Horses just don't realize that people have feelings, and they relate better to animals. Sometimes they view themselves as being more popular than they really are. Horse people generally have good health and they live long lives.

Horses are compatible with Dogs and Tigers.

(Remember that the Chinese years do not correspond exactly to the Western calendar. First look up your animal sign in the table at the beginning of this chapter).

Wood Horse (1954, 2014)

Sociable, cooperative, cheerful, high-spirited people who enjoy moving in pleasant circles. They love being in the country and love working on the land. Not city types. Not all are family people, some preferring the freedom to follow their dreams. Those who like family love are thoughtful and caring. Intelligent and inventive, they recover easily from adversity.

Fire Horse (1966, 2026)

Adventurous daredevils who love travel and sport. Restless, active, intelligent and charming, but also confrontational, revolutionary, unpredictable and unable to accept supervision. Hate commitment and discipline when young, but they may over-discipline their own children. Prosperous later if they settle to a trade or run a business of their own. They can be pretty awful in relationships. Some Fire Horses need the protection and help of their parents throughout their lives.

Earth Horse (1918, 1978)
A difficult start in life, possibly due to illness. Not much help from their families. Respectable, logical but sometimes indecisive, easygoing, friendly. They hate making decisions. Impatient and impetuous when young, but they mature well. May be bossy or tyrannical in love.

Metal Horse (1930, 1990)
Stubborn and self-centered, restless and sometimes irrational. Not easy to live with, although charming company on a social level. They seek constant change, excitement, new places, attractions and entertainment - great travelers but also very restless. Hard workers, good salesmen, strong recuperative powers after illness. Lucky, and able to live the good life with good clothes, good food, a good home and great holidays. Status seekers. They love a fight or argument. Not great marriage partners, and they may not see the need for a partner.

Water Horse (1942, 2002)
A difficult childhood in a problem household. Poverty in early life, but they become self-made successes later. Very restless, great travelers, athletic, competitive. Great talkers and listeners. Good friends, but hard to live or work with due to inconsistency. Unlikely to settle into family life.

The Goat
Yin
Goats are intelligent, studious and slightly reserved. One point that is well known in China but never commented upon in western books is that Goats can and do take on enormous amounts of work,

and they can work themselves into illness and an early grave if they are not careful. They need to be married to partners who make them take rests and holidays, rather than those who are happy to live off them or to exhaust the Goat's energies for their own benefit. They are valued in China for being patient and able to put up with almost anything. Goats are pleasant, gentle companions who can both entertain and listen to others. They take an interest in a wide variety of subjects and they are frequently drawn towards the occult. Goats are extremely sensitive to atmosphere and to the thoughts and feelings of others. Their values are spiritual rather than material, which means that they rarely envy those who have more money or possessions than they do. In some ways they are too absorbed in what they are doing to feel jealous of others, but they attract jealousy and when this happens it hurts them badly. Goats are highly intuitive and often extremely psychic, but while some of them take to these subjects easily, others are so unnerved by their abilities and their experiences that they run from them.

Usually found in the world of the arts, music, writing or in the caring professions, Goats take their work seriously and they push themselves to high standards of achievement. They may appear slightly dreamy, unpretentious and even lighthearted, but when they take on a commitment, they see it through. They have a natural respect for the dignity of others and they love children and animals. Being romantic and vulnerable, Goats don't like to wear their hearts on their sleeves. They may appear casual (even heartless) to a new lover while hiding their sensitive feelings. Goats are easily embarrassed and they would hate to be an embarrassment to others. These folk suffer when faced with cruel or confrontational people. They seem to find happiness and sometimes a soul mate later in life. Goats are always nicely turned out, and they often have a magical kind of grace and charisma, and a hint of animal magnetism.

Goats are compatible with Rabbits and Pigs.

(Remember that the Chinese years do not correspond exactly to the Western calendar. First look up your animal sign in the table at the beginning of this chapter).

Wood Goat (1955, 2015)
Respectable, decent, hard working. Their early years are fairly tough but they make good eventually. Happy to support others, especially their children. They may have unhelpful siblings and parents, but they may inherit money from them. They do better in love and marriage than other Goats, and they often have several children. Artistic, gentle, fond of nature.

Fire Goat (1907, 1967)
Dreamers and drifters, these Goats are not keen on family life or committed relationships until late in life. Their emotions tend to be unstable and their behavior bizarre. Money comes and goes. Good talkers with great ideas and enough patience to put them into action. Good teachers and diplomats.

Earth Goat (1919, 1979)
Trustworthy, straightforward, sensitive and stable, these Goats can have quite a good life. Conservative and decent, they work hard and obtain wealth through their own efforts. Sociable and clubbable, often artistic. Too honest and frank in relationships.

Metal Goat (1931, 1991)
Artistic, cultured connoisseurs whose homes and businesses are stylish and elegant. Strong emotions make these Goats hard to fathom. Sensitive, easily hurt, possessive and self-protective, they need a secure and stable life. Women are luckier and more successful than men, especially in family life. Sound business sense leads to stability and success, but smaller enterprises are luckier for them than large ones. Can be demanding in love.

Water Goat (1943, 2003)
These Goats are too nice. They need approval and they hate to upset anyone, preferring to follow the herd. They fear change and they aren't competitive or particularly ambitious.

Generous, kind and helpful, they are happy as long as they are loved. They take advantage of opportunities and they can be surprisingly successful in later life. Talented, good communicators, but modesty can hinder their success.

The Monkey
Yang

Monkeys can be great company. They are intelligent, humorous and exciting. They like to live in the fast lane with plenty of change, challenge and a stream of new faces around them. They do not cope well with routine, timetables or necessary chores and they are easily bored. They learn quickly and are intuitive to the point of clairvoyance, but being quick on the uptake themselves, they can be impatient with those who are slower to catch on. Monkeys read quickly and absorb ideas fast, but many of them prefer to gain their information from the television or the grapevine than to plough through long-winded books. Their sarcasm can be hurtful and they make formidable verbal adversaries. They are hard workers but they need to set their own goals. They never work for the approval of others, and for this reason they are probably best suited to self-employment. Monkeys frequently put other people's backs up, and they walk away from difficult situations while allowing other slower types to carry the can for them. They have an air of arrogance and they may look down on those who are not as bright or as successful as they are. Monkeys make good journalists, salespersons, advertisers and drivers. They often have excellent speaking or writing skills.

Monkeys are surprisingly successful in relationships because they really do need to love and be loved, but they haven't much patience with a weak-kneed or sickly partner. Monkeys of both sexes need a stable partner who allows them enough rope to get away with some of their tricks, while keeping a weather eye on them. They can become extremely downhearted and hurt, because there is a childlike quality about them. They are good with children and they love their own children to distraction.

They are compatible with Rats and Dragons.

(Remember that the Chinese years do not correspond exactly to the Western calendar. First look up your animal sign in the table at the beginning of this chapter).

Wood Monkey (1944, 2004)
Decent, kindly, sensible, hard working and loyal. These Monkeys can be restless when young and they may travel or live unsettled lives when young. Excellent business people who strive to meet new challenges or to bring new ideas to fruition. Inventive and creative. Later marriages are more successful. Some Wood Monkeys need to be dominated.

Fire Monkey (1956, 2016)
Forceful, domineering, enterprising, lively, passionate, unpredictable and energetic. These Monkeys are destined for success. They overcome obstacles and push others out of the way. They are business orientated, clever at making money and they can become tycoons. Sometimes a family history of loss and poverty is the motivating factor. Unpredictable in love.

Earth Monkey (1908, 1968)
Clever and hard working, fairly placid and generous to those they love, Earth Monkeys are successful as they stick to things until they come right. Intellectual, mischievous, charitable and kind to family and friends, but with little time for outsiders. Can be poor marriage partners or uncaring lovers.

Metal Monkey (1920, 1980)
These hot-blooded Monkeys are real powerhouses and financial wizards. They are ambitious and hard working, but they may direct their energies towards charitable or religious work rather than money-making schemes. Passionate and possessive in love or in beliefs.

Water Monkey (1932, 1992)
Charming, capable, attractive and smartly dressed, these Monkeys are stylish and original. They make wonderful agents and negotiators, as they are urbane and able to talk

well. Restless and great travelers. They marry well and get on with their families.

The Rooster
Yin

These outgoing, glamorous people make friends easily and enjoy being in the middle of things. They work hard, often in an inventive and original manner, but they can never hide their light under a bushel. Roosters have little time for dull-witted people or those who don't catch on to an idea quickly. They have broad minds and are often well read. Roosters can be opinionated, even boastful or conceited at times, but they never sulk or bear grudges. They can take offence quickly and give it even more quickly, but they soon forget and return to their normal cheerful natures. Although flirtatious, they are usually faithful once they settle down, and they care for their families in a responsible manner. Some Roosters make many friends but prefer to live on their own rather than sharing their precious space or their belongings with others.

Roosters have such lively minds that they love any kind of novelty. They can achieve a great deal though study and work and they hate to be kept from reaching the top of the tree. They are honest and open, courageous and outwardly confident. Roosters are original and different from others in many ways; they can be difficult to live with, but they are basically honest and decent. There is a pattern of fate or destiny that seems to haunt all Roosters, which means that their families are usually of little or no help to them, and they may even be positively destructive towards them.

Roosters are compatible with Oxen and Snakes.

(Remember that the Chinese years do not correspond exactly to the Western calendar. First look up your animal sign in the table at the beginning of this chapter).

Wood Rooster (1945, 2005)

Forward looking, clever, fair-minded and honest. These Roosters are pleasant, sociable and reliable, but they need their own way, both in business and in personal life. They can talk the hind leg off a donkey and bore everyone to death, or they may be too demanding. They earn good money because they love to spend. Creative and lively, they are great fun. Passionate when in love.

Fire Rooster (1957, 2017)
These Roosters may be born leaders, tycoons or independent types who work in the entertainment field. Hard working, intense, excitable and highly self-motivated, they are destined for success. Their early life is tough, but sooner or later they go out on their own and make a better life for themselves. Being sociable, they make friends easily. They can make money, but fate also brings them windfalls and inheritances. Not overly successful in romance or family life.

Earth Rooster (1909, 1969)
These Roosters are academic, systematic, clever, analytical and thorough. They also tend to be extremely critical and opinionated, which means that they alienate others. They are full of potential but success may evade them. They have a flair for theatre and the arts, and they can be good organizers and financial managers. In a search for emotional security, they may marry young and lumber themselves with children before their lives have properly started, but they remain caring to those whom they love.

Metal Rooster (1921, 1981)
These Roosters are destined for glittering careers, but while fame might be inevitable, fortune may not follow in great abundance. Arrogance and an abrasive self-centered attitude might cost these Roosters a lot, both in terms of career and family life; their moodiness doesn't help, but their hard work and idealism will take them far.

Water Rooster (1933, 1993)
These Roosters are at home with any form of communication, whether this be talking, working with computers, writing or organizing a business. They make excellent arbitra-

tors and lawyers, and they also appreciate art and music. Their families are no help to them, but they manage to make a good life for themselves without recourse to their families. Their finances are usually fairly good throughout life. Good to their partners and children.

The Dog
Yang

These clever, versatile people are good workers who can cope with details. They are sometimes workaholics, but they don't usually rise too highly up a promotion ladder. Dogs are intelligent, pleasant and very quick-minded, but they like to work at their own reasonable pace without being hassled by company politics. Some Dogs are so naive that they don't have much of a grip on what goes on in the business world. Dogs hate injustice or a lack of fair play. These creative people are pleasant, charming and friendly and they excel in the arts, where their discriminating eye and attention to detail can take them far. They can be critical of themselves and others, sometimes they can be abrupt and hurtful, and they lash out in a particularly sarcastic manner when they feel threatened. Dogs are a little reserved, they hate displays of emotion and they are easily embarrassed.

Dogs are good-looking and some are very good listeners. While counseling others they have a broad-minded, non-judgmental attitude, and this ability to listen makes them popular as friends and potential lovers. They are faithful in marriage and they make reliable partners, as long as they feel appreciated. They can be hard to live with because they take life seriously, and their nerves can get them down from time to time. On the whole, they put up with a great deal and they will try to do what they see as their duty. Dogs need a nice home with good quality material possessions around them. They like to look good and also to eat well-prepared, sensible food (although the Dogs that I know prefer eating out to cooking...).

Dogs are compatible with Tigers and Horses.

(Remember that the Chinese years do not correspond exactly to the Western calendar. First look up your animal sign in the table at the beginning of this chapter).

Wood Dog (1934, 1994)

These pleasant Dogs balance ambition against a fairly spiritual attitude. They may be a little too dependent upon their families. They enjoy travelling and home projects such as do-it-yourself jobs and gardening. Wood Dogs need to guard against theft or being taken advantage of by employees. They love to talk, work and to make money. Women make good wives who can earn good money in their own right.

Fire Dog (1946, 2006)

Charming, adventurous, generous, honest and dramatic. These Dogs are destined to have charmed lives. They can make a success of almost anything, and their family and love lives are easy and pleasant. They enjoy travel. They can attack or rebel if pushed too far, and they can be protective of their reputations or their families.

Earth Dog (1958, 2018)

These Dogs make steady workers and organized thinkers, but they may do more than is strictly necessary. Careful, cautious, secretive and creative, but sometimes silly over money. Their early lives are difficult and they can be short of money through their own fecklessness, but they learn to manage better later on. Better with things than with people. Not much inclined to romance.

Metal Dog (1910, 1970)

These strong characters can become leaders of men, and while some are critical tyrants who take offence easily, others are cheerful and pleasant. They are much better at family life than outsiders would believe them to be, and they are very faithful and loyal to lovers and friends. They move in high places, mix with top people and they may work as assistants to such people. Metal Dogs can fight for causes.

Water Dog (1922, 1982)
These easygoing Dogs enjoy family life and they may spend their lives helping others. They have many friends, they travel widely and they do interesting work. They can be too restless to settle down until later in life. Their early years are not wonderful, but they attract help from influential people and usually end up doing quite well. They communicate feelings easily and they need loyal and understanding lovers.

The Pig
Yin
Pigs have an outwardly gentle and retiring attitude that belies their quick minds and stubborn determination. They may appear to be easily taken in, but this is not so. Pigs are honest, reasonable, hard working, kindly and sincere. They hate trickery and dishonesty, and they cannot understand advantage-takers. They think and read deeply, and they have a philosophical turn of mind. They enjoy art, music and culture. Pigs can do well in positions of reasonable responsibility, but they may not be able enough or ambitious enough for a true executive position. They are dutiful, intelligent and capable, and they don't make unnecessary waves because they prefer to keep their opinions to themselves. Although generous to loved ones, they can be stingy to themselves and they love to get the full use out of anything. Garage, boot and jumble sales draw Pigs like a magnet. Pigs are quite shy and they prefer to keep their troubles to themselves.

Pigs need a change of scene from time to time and they value their freedom, so they don't like being questioned as to their intentions or even their whereabouts. They are intensely loyal to their families and their small circle of friends. They make devoted, faithful partners and very loving parents. Their resilience allows them to bounce back from illness or problems so that they continue their steady and fairly unambitious progress through life. Pigs make good administrators but they may have some difficult in dealing with people due to their reserve. Many Pigs are extremely sensual and very highly sexed. Some of them take this too far.

They are compatible with Rabbits and Goats.

(Remember that the Chinese years do not correspond exactly to the Western calendar. First look up your animal sign in the table at the beginning of this chapter).

Wood Pig (1935, 1995)

Wood Pigs may have health problems early in life and/or they may be destined to have difficult children. Home and family life can be pleasant but not always easy or convenient, although this is a very important area of their lives into which they put a great deal of effort. Charitable and sociable, and they work best in a field that allows them to deal with the public or to organize large-scale events. Their sensuality can get them into trouble.

Fire Pig (1947, 2007)

Difficulties early in life give way to considerable success later on. Optimistic and independent, these Pigs can succeed at anything they attempt. Great entertainers. Their strong sensuality may lead to affairs, but if they can hold this in check, they enjoy family life. They can benefit from windfalls. They are happy if they can combine work and home life.

Earth Pig (1959, 2019)

These Pigs are family minded and they sacrifice much for their families. It is usually better for them to have children later rather than earlier. They are quite clever and they like to read. Earth Pigs are patient and persistent, and they usually make enough money to provide themselves with quality goods. They are clannish and they may be quite unpleasant to those who are not related to them. They love to impress others.

Metal Pig (1911, 1971)

These strong personalities can bulldoze their way through life, frightening others into doing their will, but this does not ultimately serve them well. Some Metal Pigs manage to live without making undue trouble for themselves or others. Well organized, structured, ambitious and sociable, they can reach the very top, especially if they deal in land or property. A late marriage would be successful.

Water Pig (1923, 1983)

Ambition and perseverance leads these Pigs to the top of the tree and they end their lives in considerable comfort. Oddly enough, these Pigs like to think well of others and they can be gullible. Some are very charitable and more interested in being happy and making others happy than in money, while others are ambitious and money-minded. These Pigs seem to be all-or-nothing types. Affectionate, caring and good with children.

The elements in Chinese astrology

Despite the fact that we in the west are so attracted to the charm of the zodiac animals, the elements are in many ways more important to the Chinese, because they represent the heavenly plane of activity rather than the earthly one. The Chinese consider the elements to be a kind of shorthand that shows the way that the influences of heaven work here on earth. This thinking is similar to the way that old time astrologers in the west saw the influence of heaven working through the planets and affecting people and events on earth. An imbalance in the elements in a horoscope is said to be responsible for certain ailments or particularly difficult life situations. For example, if Fire dominates the chart, this will cause illnesses such as heart attacks, strokes, fevers and outbreaks of rashes or other eruptive ailments, while an overabundance of Water is responsible for water retention or rheumatism.

The order of the elements is:

1 Wood
2 Fire
3 Earth
4 Metal
5 Water
Each element rules a consecutive two-year period.

The Chinese link the elements to five of the planets:
Wood is linked to Jupiter
Fire is linked to Mars
Earth is linked to Saturn
Metal is linked to Venus
Water is linked to Mercury

A western astrologer would have no argument with the linking of Fire to Mars and Earth to Saturn, but he would find the concept of Water and Mercury a strange one. Wood and Metal don't exist in the western system, while the western element of Air doesn't exist in Chinese astrology. When one looks a little more closely at the elements, the two systems can become compatible. Metal people are said to be stubborn and also money-minded, and to Westerners Venus is associated with Taurus and Libra, which are also notoriously stubborn signs that are also fond of the good life. The Chinese see the element of Water as ruling communications rather than emotions, so the attachment to Mercury also works. The association of Wood with Jupiter is a little more difficult, but the Chinese consider that Wood represents the east, the sun rise and springtime, so the optimism associated with Jupiter fits this element well.

In the west, we are accustomed to the names Wood, Fire, Metal, Earth and Water, but the following variations are also used:
Wood can be called Trees.
Earth can be called Soil.
Metal can be Iron, Steel or Gold.
Water can also be called Torrent.

The lucky creatures listed in the references that follow are the Tortoise, Dragon, Phoenix (or any other bird), Tiger and Emperor. Two of these are the same as the animals of the Chinese zodiac, but this is purely coincidental.
The elemental creatures in the lists rule compass points or directions, their origins are ancient, and they have no connection to the astrology year animals.

The element years

Finding the element for your year of birth is easy. Take the year of your birth and look at the number that it ended in, then check out below the element for your year of birth. For example, someone born in 1987 would have been born in a Fire year; someone born in 1941 would have been born in a Metal year.

Years ending in 4 or 5: Wood
Years ending in 6 or 7: Fire
Years ending in 8 or 9: Earth

Years ending in 0 or 1: Metal

Years ending in 2 or 3: Water

NB: Some people who were born in the months of January and early February may have been born before the Chinese New year, which means that they may belong to the previous year. Check back in the Astro Year section to find the date of the Chinese New Year in your birth year.

This is very important; it explains why some people mistake their details in Chinese astrology and find that their supposed characteristics don't fit them at all!

Now let us move on to the character readings for each of the elements, bearing in mind that these are more accurate and more meaningful than those for the animal year signs.

Active and receptive elements

You will notice that each element is described in general and then broken down into Active or Receptive.

The elements in astrology are neither Yang nor Yin, but a Yang animal always rules the first year in a two-year element block or binomial, and this turns the element into an active one.

The second year is always ruled by a Yin animal, which turns the element into a receptive one. For example:

1970: Dog, Yang, Active Metal.

1971: Pig, Yin, Receptive Metal.

Wood

Connections

When active	Oak
When receptive	Willow
Territory (Active)	Intellect
Territory (Receptive)	Knowledge
Seeks	Wisdom
Comportment	Achiever
Body shape (Active)	Raw-boned
Body shape (Receptive)	Slender
Helped by	Water
Hindered by	Metal
Lucky day	Thursday
Lucky season	Spring
Lucky planet	Jupiter
Lucky color	Green
Lucky direction	East
Lucky shape	Rectangle
Lucky creature	Dragon

In ancient times, Wood people were the intellectuals who went into astronomy, astrology, philosophy, teaching and the law. Some were healers and diviners who knew how to interpret oracles. These days, Wood folk gravitate to computers, electronics, science, communications and centers of learning.

These people are either given educational opportunities at a young age or they seek out training and education for themselves later on. Some are idealists who try to improve the lot of others, but some are unrealistic or unworldly. Many are intellectuals who prefer to use their minds rather than to work with their hands, while others assist communications by working in some form of transportation. Even today, many Wood people are interested in religion, spirituality or philosophy.

Wood people have high standards, strong morals and ethics and they often have a strong belief in themselves. They have a natural sense of the value of everything, they know instinctively what will work for them, and this can lead them into executive positions in their chosen careers.

Wood people can attract others to their causes. In business, they like to join forces with others in order to create large-scale operations with many different products or facets, because focusing on one product or service bores them. Wood people flourish in a corporate environment and they know how many beans make five, but they can expand too far, take on too much and thus find it hard to control either their business or their personal lives.

These folk are cooperative and considerate towards others and they are compassionate and caring. All the Wood types that I have come across are generous to others and bad at keeping money by for a rainy day. When times of trouble come around and they need some help for themselves, they are astounded to discover that others are not happy to return their generosity or kindness.

Active Wood - The Oak
Rat, Tiger, Dragon, Horse, Monkey and Dog.

These people are intelligent, realistic, astute and they see through to the truth of a matter. They are quite ambitious and hard working, but their achievements are rarely made at the expense of others. Honest and dependable, but also reserved and independent, they beaver away quietly and achieve the goals that they set themselves.

These well-organized folk can lead a team or work alone. They are self-motivated, and those who rely upon their judgement trust them. They thrive in any field that requires a clever and well-organized mind, such as medicine, science, computer-aided design, publishing and writing.

The key to these people's success is that they are honest, trustworthy, ethical and responsible, and they inspire trust in others.

Romantically speaking, the Active Wood type is honest and straightforward. Neither sex plays games, but they need to be left alone to do things the way they think is right, and they cannot be dictated to.

Receptive Wood - The Willow
Ox, Rabbit, Snake, Goat, Rooster and Pig.

These laid-back personalities can be walked over, because they are so in-tune with the needs of others that they neglect their own. Receptive Wood types can become deeply involved with a cause, and they can be left behind in the race for success and achievement as a result. They are used and then neglected or discarded by others who are cleverer at company politics and whose personal ambition is stronger. If these people can find a good business partner or a good boss to work for, they can be very happy and successful.

They make wonderful back-room boys, whose expertise is necessary to an end result. Suitable careers include almost anything that can be done with a computer, such as systems analysis, financial tables, data analysis, research, librarian, editor, designer, typesetter, biographer, critic, video and music editor or technician. Some will work for religious, spiritual or charitable organizations while others choose psychology, psychiatry, preparing courses for self-improvement or management training.

They are pleased when their abilities are recognized and rewarded by a good boss. They don't ask for recognition, but so often they invent the systems that make things work, only to find that someone else takes the credit.

Needless to say, in matters of romance, the Receptive Wood types are real softies. They may not have the confidence to go after the one they fancy, and they wait for others to notice their devotion. Men woo their lover in romantic ways with flowers and gifts, but they don't know how to sweep her off her feet. Women are loving, gentle and great mothers, but they can be dumped if a determined predator comes along and snatches their man away from them.

Fire

Connections

When active	Blaze
When receptive	Flame
Territory (Active)	Activity
Territory (Receptive)	Enterprise
Seeks	Fame
Comportment	Showman
Body shape (Active)	Powerful
Body shape (Receptive)	Wiry
Helped by	Wood
Hindered by	Water
Lucky day	Tuesday
Lucky season	Summer
Lucky planet	Mars
Lucky color	Vermilion
Lucky direction	South
Lucky shape	Triangle
Lucky creature	Phoenix

In ancient China, Fire people belonged to the warrior class, defending the Emperor and the empire. They were also entertainers, acrobats, athletes and those who put on parades and public events.

In the modern world, such folk would be active as full or part time members of the armed forces, the police, the fire service and the ambulance service. They might be explorers, rangers, adventurers, bandits and even travelers in space. They are comfortable with the technology of their times, but they put it to practical use rather than invent and explore on an intellectual level. Other fire types are to be found in show business, as actors, entertainers or sports personalities, but they may also be politicians and union bosses.

These people want to be seen and to be known, and while they may be idealistic when fighting for a cause, they are also personally ambitious. They are confrontational, short fused, courageous and sometimes reckless. They can be cruel and unfeeling. Some Fire types become top criminals!

Fire people are the leaders of the pack. They make excellent military leaders because they are decisive, courageous and self-confident, but they can go too far and become aggressive and reckless. These people are creative and not short of an idea or two, and they can rally others to their cause, but they may forget that not everyone is as addicted to risk-taking as they are. They love movement and change, and their restless natures mean that they are never still for long. Fire people can gamble, either in the literal sense or by taking chances in life. They love a challenge and they tend not to see potential pitfalls before plunging ahead.

These dynamic, pioneering, impulsive and outspoken folk certainly get things moving, but they can make enemies and they can be the architects of their own downfall. Impatience and irritability may be their acknowledged faults, but without such pioneering and courageous "brave-hearts" in the world, there would be little progress.

Active fire - The Blaze
Rat, Tiger, Dragon, Horse, Monkey and Dog.

These powerful characters have a hot temperament and they don't have the patience to work around a situation. They are open and direct. They are quick and clever and they can't always be bothered to study a subject in depth or to work hard at anything. They speak out and they don't wait for anything or anybody.

Their chosen field is anything that requires courage and action, and they can become the hero or heroine of the hour. They talk well and they can make determined sales people, lawyers or actors. Others don't easily put them off and they plough their way through difficulties. Active Fire people can find work in the military or similar fields, also exploration of oil, minerals or other resources. They enjoy public life and they make wonderful action heroes on stage or in film. According to one source that I have found, they are said to be excellent chefs, due to the Chinese association with flames and ovens.

Romantically speaking, the Active Fire types are charming, seductive, flirtatious and passionate. They make great lovers but they don't necessarily stay around for long or make a faithful commitment to anyone. The women can settle into relationships, albeit confrontational ones.

Receptive Fire - The Flame
Ox, Rabbit, Snake, Goat, Rooster and Pig.

The Receptive Fire type is far less interested in militarism or adventure than the Active type. This is the showman or woman who finds work in the entertainment field of stage, screen or even a circus or rodeo. This is the rhinestone cowboy, and also sometimes a smooth talking confidence trickster. Success can also be found in advertising, sales, marketing, public relations, journalism and public speaking or in artistic or musical areas such as singing or playing music. Window-dressing, painting murals and putting on events and festivals might appeal. Receptive Fire types know how to appeal to the public mood.

Romantically speaking, these passionate folk will stay with a partner who can meet their needs for sex and excitement. They seek a spiritual soul mate. Women are attractive and feminine, but they need a career and the freedom to come and go as they please. Neither sex can stand an unfaithful partner, and both sexes can become violent and confrontational.

Earth

Connections	
When active	Grassland
When receptive	Farm
Territory (Active)	Industry
Territory (Receptive)	Services
Seeks	Security
Comportment	Still
Body shape (Active)	Stocky
Body shape (Receptive)	Stocky
Helped by	Fire
Hindered by	Wood
Lucky day	Saturday
Lucky season	The equinoxes
Lucky planet	Saturn
Lucky color	Yellow
Lucky direction	Center
Lucky shape	Square
Lucky creature	The Emperor

In ancient China, Earth people were the builders of temples, palaces and important buildings, and also the farmers, shepherds and trainers of water buffaloes.

In the modern world, the domain of Earth people is much the same, being that of construction, manufacturing, food production, farming, ecology, veterinary work and medicine. Earth people can be very tuned into nature or to large-scale trends. These people may also find work as food processors, chefs, caterers and hotel managers. They usually do well in their chosen professions, and they will either own a farm or business, or they will rise to an executive position in someone else's. They prefer to stay put and develop something than to move around much or to change direction. They are sensible, reliable and realistic. Their nature is placid, slow to anger but also slow to forget a hurt. They have excellent brains and they can be shrewd in business matters.

Earth people are practical, methodical and organized, and they create the solid foundations upon which any enterprise is built. These people make excellent executives, administrators, farmers and accountants, and they have a firm grip on what will and what will not work. They can foresee trends and they have a talent for large scale and long-term planning, all of which makes them excellent government and civil workers, lawyers and bankers.

Earth people are generous and loving to their families, and their relaxed manner makes for a pleasant home atmosphere.

Active Earth - The Grassland
Rat, Tiger, Dragon, Horse, Monkey or Dog.

These responsible and decent people live within the conventions of the society that they inhabit. Their executive abilities, capacity for hard work, shrewdness, talent for leadership and ambition can lead to them to positions of wealth and honor. They can be ruthless, tough minded and sometimes unfair in the pursuit of their goals. They might work in the timber industry, mining, engineering, farming, forestry and real estate. Other lines include banking, home-loans, insurance, home security and finance. Active Earth people go where the power is, and then ensure that they stay put long enough to reach the top. Such matters as the preservation of our planet or ecology would appeal, either as a job or a sideline. Oddly enough, athletics - especially those sports that require strength - can also appeal to these types.

Romantically speaking, Active Earth men are often very successful with women. They can offer them security and a good lifestyle, but they are also sensual and passionate lovers. They are not terribly romantic, but they are reliable. Women of this type are reliable, sensible and motherly, and they prefer a settled commitment to experimenting with a variety of lovers. They are great mothers and homemakers, and they need a decent, lasting, relationship.

Receptive Earth - The Farm
Ox, Rabbit, Snake, Goat, Rooster and Pig.

Most Receptive Earth types are hard working and successful, but some are negative, suspicious, overcautious and awkward, and they can refuse to do anything beyond the immediate scope of their job description. Nicer Receptive Earth types are reliable workers who find jobs that suit their abilities, and in which they can stay over the years. They are capable and efficient, if perhaps a little slow at times. They have a talent for creating attractive things so they might go in for interior decorating, ceramics, pottery, house building, landscape gardening or looking after a golf club or sports ground. They may work in animal husbandry or in a zoo, alternatively in engineering, shipping, road or rail transport and haulage. Hobbies might include archaeology, marine biology, geology or other solid sciences, and, of course, land preservation and ecology.

They need emotional security and they prefer to stick with one reliable partner. They are sensual lovers.

Metal

Connections	
When active	Steel
When receptive	Ornament
Territory (Active)	Management
Territory (Receptive)	The arts
Seeks	Status
Comportment	Graceful
Body shape (Active)	Balanced
Body shape (Receptive)	Curvaceous
Helped by	Earth
Hindered by	Fire
Lucky day	Friday
Lucky season	Autumn
Lucky planet	Venus
Lucky color	White
Lucky direction	West & North West
Lucky shape	Oval, circle
Lucky creature	Tiger

In ancient China, the Metal element was associated with the Emperor and with his civil servants and administrators, lawyers and top religious leaders. However, metal also referred to talented artists, dancers, poets, writers, composers, sculptors and those who looked after galleries, opera houses and other places where creative talents were displayed. In some cases, metal referred to courtiers and those who were wealthy enough to be collectors, admirers of art and even amusing hangers-on and "wannabes" who had the time and money to be seen around in all the best places. These people may have been born rich, or they will rise in status through luck or good management.

Such modern personalities as film stars, photographers, fashion designers and supermodels could be included among the Metal types. In short, these people turn their artistic, creative or managerial talents to good use through a combination of hard work, focused ambitions and plain good luck. Many are charming, witty, good looking or just plain lucky - as we in the west would say, born with a silver spoon in their mouths. Even here the metal theme seeps through.

Metal people have determined and independent personalities, and they are hard to influence. Once they have decided upon a course of action, they stick to it. This tenacity ensures that they can often turn a slow-starting enterprise into an eventual success, but the downside of their stubbornness is that they find it difficult to let go of a situation once it has become untenable. Their desire to have their own way stands them in good stead, as long as their vision of what will succeed is right, but it can lead to disaster when their hunches are off-center.

These people don't brook interference, even when it is meant kindly, and their supreme independence means that they prefer to handle problems by themselves. Metal people often have a good grasp of financial matters.

Active Metal - The Steel
Rat, Tiger, Dragon, Horse, Monkey or Dog.

These people look the part. They are respected and admired, and they may even put on a few airs and graces. They love to appear conservative and to be respected, and they create an aura of money or status that is sometimes hard for them to sustain. Active Metal people may be born into families that give them the tools for success. Many come from stable backgrounds where they are given educational opportunities and are exposed to literature, music and the arts in addition to maths and the sciences. Those who don't have such great childhood experiences still make their way to the top. These folk love positions of power and status, and many adore the symbols of that status; not only big houses and cars but also military insignia, Masonic accoutrements and the symbol of the Chamber of Commerce on their paperwork.

Just as in ancient China, Active Metal types can be found in politics, the civil service, executive industrial positions, or as respected leaders in the art world. Whether in civil engineering, running an airline or putting on fashion shows, everything is done on a large scale. When Active Metal people have to start from the bottom they move upwards very quickly. This is partly due to talent or executive abilities, but it is also due to hard work and their habit of focusing very directly upon their chosen goals.

These people are only really happy at the top of the heap, where they inspire loyal and hardworking subordinates, and where they can delegate the more mundane aspects of their work.

Romantically speaking, Active Metal men are good looking and attractive to women. They can be very determined once they have set their sights on a potential partner, but they become bored with them very quickly and they soon move on. In troubled relationships, they become physically and mentally abusive, and they can be cruel and unfeeling.

Women of this element are very demanding. They pursue the man they fancy, and the guy must toe the line or suffer the consequences. In today's atmosphere of short-lived relationships, such women soon find themselves alone, unless they can learn to hold back on criticism and to modify their behavior.

Receptive Metal - The Ornament
Ox, Rabbit, Snake, Goat, Rooster, Pig.

While still belonging to the realm of Metal, this is a much softer type of personality, but there is still a desire to reach the top of the tree and also a degree of obstinate determination. However, this personality is gentler than the Active Metal type. Some Receptive Metal types fight for fair play and initiate political movements, and they can get bees in their bonnets about some cause or other due to their strong sense of justice. They are innovators and sometimes inventors, and they enjoy discovering and promoting new products or services. Receptive Metal folk are friendly and diplomatic, gentle and pleasant in public, but in private situations they can be critical and unfeeling.

These people are drawn to the world of the arts, dancing, photography, fashion, jewelry or music, and they may open shops or businesses that deal with these products. They may have a talent for the creation of beauty, and they certainly appreciate it. Receptive Metal people can dress a window or entertain a celebrity in the best of style - they bring beauty to everything that they touch. Women may become involved in show business as dancers, even exotic dancers, and they may become hostesses - either in the sense of putting on events and entertaining at home, or of the other kind who use their charm as escorts to powerful men.

Romantically, the males guard against being hurt or rejected, and they may prefer an open-ended relationship to a true commitment. They appear romantic, remembering birthdays and sending flowers, but they take care to preserve their independence. This behavior puzzles their girlfriends, because they look as though they care but their behavior is designed purely to ensure that they are always in demand. In extreme cases, they tend to love themselves far more than they can ever love another.

Women of this element seek a man with money and status. If the man can't give this woman the lifestyle she wants, he won't get anywhere with her.

Water

Connections	
When active	River
When receptive	Fishing net
Territory (Active)	Liquid assets
Territory (Receptive)	Fixed assets
Seeks	Wealth
Comportment	Flexible
Body shape (Active)	Rounded
Body shape (Receptive)	Rounded
Helped by	Metal
Hindered by	Earth
Lucky day	Wednesday
Lucky season	Winter
Lucky planet	Mercury
Lucky color	Black
Lucky direction	North
Lucky shape	Wavy lines
Lucky creature	Tortoise

Water people were the directors of finance. They looked after the Imperial Treasury and they were tax collectors, storage and warehouse stewards, merchants, landlords, bankers and those who connived and bribed in order to influence people who mattered. They controlled the finances and allocated budgets to other government departments.

These are intuitive people who can spot a trend before it arrives and they are happy to encourage others to use their talents to good advantage. Water people live in a world of creativity and ideas, but they are also quite practical because they have the knack of turning ideas into concrete reality. Their intuitive talent for hitting on the right idea at the right time, coupled with their salesmanship, ensures that they can create a market when none existed before. Water people know how to find the right contacts and avenues for success and they can find ways of making things work for them.

However, they dislike direct confrontation and they will always endeavor to find a way round difficulties rather than to face them head on. These people can be bullied at times and they may make the mistake of leaning too heavily on stronger personalities. Today, Water people tend to work in banking, finance, foreign exchange, the stock markets, home loans, credit schemes, insurance and so forth. Some are cashiers or bookkeepers and others are bookmakers. They may raise money for a cause or handle money on behalf of others. They know how to make money, even when times are hard. If they lose money, they usually find a way of making it back again. Despite their considerable financial skills, Water people are gentle souls who like to help others. Some are artistic or creative and many of them enjoy music and dancing, but many put on weight in later life if they are not careful.

A very Chinese way of viewing matters related to water is that of communications. Thus modern day telephone, email, faxes and such things as air travel, radio and television come under the rulership of this element. This makes sense when one considers that in ancient times the best way to travel any distance was by river and canal, and the main towns were always situated on rivers. Goods moved around the country by water.

Active Water - The River
Rat, Tiger, Dragon, Horse, Monkey or Dog.

These people are clever and talented and they work very hard, indeed they sometimes don't know when to stop working. They have excellent public relations skills and their natural tact and diplomacy allow them to defuse difficult situations.

Active Water people often get on well in life due to their hard work and their ability to see an opportunity and turn it into something concrete. They tune in to the public mood and fulfil a need or fill a gap in the market. Others trust them to support and finance their schemes. Their knack for finance means that they can plan and build a business from scratch or turn an ailing one around. Many are successful in publishing or in some form of financial services. Active Water people like to accumulate money and to make it grow, and they try to keep something in the bank against hard times. Romantically, Active Water men enjoy playing the field and they can date a number of women at the same time without committing to any of them. Some are quite promiscuous. Women also lead a very active sex-life and they may choose younger men, whom they teach and guide, or sometimes older men in positions of authority who can teach them about money and business.

Receptive Water - The Fishing Net
Ox, Rabbit, Snake, Goat, Rooster and Pig.

This is a far softer and gentler type than the Active Water type. These people are intuitive and kindly, but they have a knack for business and finance, although they are more likely to work for someone else than to go it alone. When Receptive Water people find a mentor in a position of authority to encourage them, they can be extremely successful.

Their marketing and financial skills take them a long way and their ability to find a market where one didn't previously exist can make them very successful. Some work in banking or accountancy while others may choose sales and marketing, due to their ability to tap into current trends and the needs of the public.

They need luck and they need to stay on the right side of the law. They work hard, sometimes too hard, and sometimes for little appreciation or reward. These people can be bullied or maltreated over a period of time, but they can take their tormentors by surprise, by finally losing their temper or more likely by simply walking out and leaving them.

Receptive Water people hide their true feelings, and this makes them hard to fathom out. They pull back from saying what is really bothering them, because they hate to cause a row, and when they do fight they become so terribly distressed that they end up worse off than if they had simply kept to their usual routine of putting up with things. Those who work or live with Receptive Water people may never really understand them.

Receptive Water males are very romantic. They may choose an older woman who is worldlier than them, or they may date many women as friends rather than committed lovers. When they fall in love, they are sincere and loyal and they hate being parted from a loved one. Females have a kind of animal magnetism and they can appear to offer sex when what they really need is a combination of love, respect, security, deep affection - and sex. Some get used and hurt by their lovers and others are seen as no more than sexual playthings.

Forecasting

Despite the current popularity of books that suggest that this or that year will be good for Horses, bad for Roosters etc., serious Chinese consultants don't rely on this kind of astrology for forecasting events. They either use the highly complex Four Pillars system or they use the relatively easy but accurate Lo Shu.

Having said this, the elements relate to each other in a way that allows a harmonizing effect in some years and a destructive one in others. For instance, a two-year spell that repeats your own birth element is considered to be active and successful, while one that precedes or follows your own is also good, but a year that is two elements away from your own is no good at all. The following list shows the system in action.

Wood element people

Active years:	Wood years.
Harmonious years:	Water and Fire years.
Difficult years:	Earth and Metal years.

Fire element people

Active years:	Fire years.
Harmonious years:	Wood and Earth years.
Difficult years:	Metal and Water years.

Earth element people

Active years:	Earth years.
Harmonious years:	Fire and Metal years.
Difficult years:	Water and Wood years.

Metal element people

Action years:	Metal years.
Harmonious years:	Earth and Water years.
Difficult years:	Wood and Fire years.

Water element people

Active years:	Water years.
Harmonious years:	Metal and Wood years.
Difficult years:	Fire and Earth years.

As you move into the part of this book that deals with the seasons and months of the year, you will discover that these are also ruled by the familiar five elements. You will soon find that in addition to particular two-year periods (binomials) being good or bad for you, certain months tend to be beneficial or difficult. For example, some people routinely have a rotten Christmas and a good time during some other month. A couple of years ago, we worked out that in the years before I knew him, my husband always moved house or changed job in February. We have recently bought a new house ourselves and oddly enough, the date that we took possession was the 29th of February!

The seasons and the months

It is easy to work out the sign and element for your season and the month, and once you have done so you will see that this adds much to the information you already have on the animal and element for your year.

The ancient Chinese year is divided up into the four seasons of spring, summer, autumn and winter. Spring is said to start more or less at the beginning of the Chinese year. The date for this is taken from the old Imperial date for New Year, which is always 4th February. This means that these seasonal divisions are a little different from our familiar western ones.

Season	Months
Spring	February, March and April
Summer	May, June and July
Autumn	August, September and October
Winter	November, December and January

Minor complications set in, because although there are four seasons there are five elements. The Chinese divide each season into three months and then they assign the first two months to one element and the third month to the element of earth, and they do this with all four of the seasons. The table below shows how this works.

Season	Month	Element
Spring	February	Wood
Spring	March	Wood
Spring	April	Earth
Summer	May	Fire
Summer	June	Fire
Summer	July	Earth
Autumn	August	Metal
Autumn	September	Metal
Autumn	October	Earth
Winter	November	Water

| Winter | December | Water |
| Winter | January | Earth |

Now let us look at the months before attaching them to their seasons. Somewhere over the centuries, a monthly calendar was imposed upon the original Chinese systems. What is known is that at some point in history, the monthly calendar became attached to the Chinese animal zodiac. Logically, one would expect the year to begin in February with the first sign of the Chinese zodiac which is the Rat, but the year actually starts with the third sign (the Tiger) and then works its way through all the signs in order

Month	Animal
February	Tiger
March	Rabbit
April	Dragon
May	Snake
June	Horse
July	Goat
August	Monkey
September	Rooster
October	Dog
November	Pig
December	Rat
January	Ox

Combining the months and the seasons

This is where we pick up the seasons again and combine them with the months, this time including the elements, Chinese zodiac animals and the Yang/Yin characteristics.

A Table of the Seasons and the Months

Spring			Summer		
Feb	Mar	Apr	May	Jun	Jul
Wood	Wood	Earth	Fire	Fire	Earth
Tiger	Rabbit	Dragon	Snake	Horse	Goat
Yang	Yin	Yang	Yin	Yang	Yin
Autumn			**Winter**		
Aug	Sep	Oct	Nov	Dec	Jan
Metal	Metal	Earth	Water	Water	Earth
Monkey	Rooster	Dog	Pig	Rat	Ox
Yang	Yin	Yang	Yin	Yang	Yin

Working from the table, this means that a person born in May would be born in the season of summer, with the element of Fire accompanied by the sign of the Snake. To find out what all this means, simply turn back a few pages and read up about the year of the Snake and then the element of Receptive Fire. Why Receptive Fire? The element becomes receptive when coupled to a sign that is Yin in character - as is the Snake. When coupled with a Yang sign, the element is considered to be Active. The elements themselves are neutral, being neither Yang nor Yin in Chinese astrology

The hour sign

Chinese astrology also includes the hour sign. The Chinese suggest that this reveals the real inner personality, the one that is often carefully hidden from view. In fact, the nature of the hour sign personality is frequently right out in the open.

Some western astrologers refer to this as a Chinese rising sign, because like the western astrological rising sign, it moves through each zodiac sign during the course of a day, but it isn't really a rising sign in the sense that western astrologers know it. The Chinese method comes from early attempts at dividing up a day into useful two-hour segments.

Find your time zone

As with anything to do with Chinese astrology, we run into complications. Most modern Chinese astrologers tell us to take the time of birth as it is at the location of birth, but older sources suggest that the birth time should be converted to Beijing time.

If you decide to stick with the local time of birth for your hour sign, you will only need to consider whether the birth occurred during daylight saving or British Summer Time, as this means subtracting an hour from the time of birth.

If you want to follow older and more accurate sources of Chinese information, you will need to adjust the time of birth to Beijing time.

Astrologers in the west are accustomed to the fact that everything has to be calculated for the Greenwich Meridian, and thus for Greenwich Mean Time (GMT). Before casting a horoscope, all local times and daylight saving schemes must be converted to GMT.

However, to the ancient Chinese, the center of the world was not Greenwich, it was Beijing! Let's face it, five or six thousand years ago, Greenwich was hardly the metropolitan center of naval navigation and accurate clock making that it became in the 18th century!

British people born when GMT was in operation need to add eight hours to the birth time, while for births when British Summer Time was in operation, only seven hours need be added. In the rare case of those born around the time of the Second World War when Double Summer Time was in operation, only six hours need be added.

Those born in other parts of the world will need to look up an atlas to find the time zone in their part of the world, and then adjust their birth time to Beijing time.

If you want to do this but you find the concept difficult, why not take this book along to a decent western astrologer and ask for help? Present day astrologers all use sophisticated software that automatically converts all birth times in all parts of the world to Greenwich Mean Time - even taking into account such things as local Daylight Saving schemes. Once they have done this, it is a matter of simply adding eight hours to bring Greenwich Mean Time forward to Beijing time.

I happen to be writing this piece of text on the first day of the new millennium. Like everyone else in the world, after going out to a party and drinking enough champagne to give me a headache, I sat and watched the replay of the celebrations on Sky Television. The presenters showed the new millennium arriving in one country after another, starting at Millennium Island in the Pacific and ending at Samoa on the other side of the date line in the Pacific during the course of 24 hours. The way the celebrations circled the earth will give you a good idea of how time changes as the earth turns.

Once you have worked out your birth time, either by using Beijing time or local time, look at the following list to see which animal rules the hour of your birth, and then look back to the characteristics of the animal to see what the hour means.

The list of hour signs

11pm to 1am	Rat
1am to 3am	Ox
3am to 5am	Tiger
5am to 7am	Rabbit
7am to 9am	Dragon
9am to 11am	Snake
11am to 1pm	Horse
1pm to 3pm	Goat
3pm to 5pm	Monkey
5pm to 7pm	Rooster
7pm to 9pm	Dog
9pm to 11pm	Pig

Having tried out the system with both local and Beijing time on many people, I find that the Beijing time reading is the accurate one. I strongly recommend that you use the Beijing time, but by all means, try out both and compare the results.

Technical information and additional explanations

For those of you who enjoy looking behind the obvious, I'll try to explain some of the origins and the thinking behind the Chinese astrology system. This chapter is fairly technical.

The heavens and the calendar

Western and Indian astrology rely upon the movement of the earth, sun, the planets and the stars around the heavens, and while the two systems do take different routes here and there, it is not too difficult for either type of astrologer to switch between the systems. Chinese astrology is very different, and a better term might be "chronology", because it derives more from the discovery of methods of measuring time here on earth than from celestial movements. Having said that, the origins of the subject did come from sky-watchers, and in particular from the constellation called the Great Bear plus the stars, Polaris and Vega.

There are still ancient calendar systems around today that are used for religious purposes in various parts of the world. In China, the modern Gregorian calendar was only instituted nationally after the communist revolution of 1949. The Chinese calendar that was in use before that date depended upon a combination of the length of reign of whatever emperor was in power, and/or an ancient form of solar and lunar calendar. Even today, Chinese farmers take the ancient calendar into account, and some Chinese even date the present time from the start of the Chinese communist "empire" in 1949. This means that our millennial year would be counted as the 51st year of the communist reign.

Variations in animal names

China is a big country with a long history, and this combination of time and geography has brought about differences in terminology from one time or place to another. In addition to this, the various Europeans who translated the names of the zodiac animals from Chinese have themselves brought about slight variations. The list that follows covers all the variations that I have discovered so far, but I am sure that there are yet more to be found in some of the older translations.

Name variations

The Rabbit:	The Hare, the Cat.
The Goat:	The Sheep, occasionally the Ram.
The Ox:	The Buffalo, and sometimes the Cow.
The Pig:	The Boar.
The Rat:	The Mouse.
The Snake:	The Serpent.
The Rooster:	The Cockerel, the Cock, the Fowl, the Hen or the Chicken.

The Chinese don't necessarily see the characteristics of these animals in the way Westerners see them. For example, the Chinese Rabbit is seen as the "super cool dude" of the zodiac rather than the timid creature that we in the west consider it to be. The Snake is considered to be vain and fond of warmth and comfort rather than cold, slimy or treacherous. The Goat (or Sheep) is considered to be shrewd, hard working and capable of putting up with a lot.

The Chinese New Year

The Chinese calendar system is based on the movement of the moon as well as that of the sun. Rather like the dates of Easter, Jewish New Year or any other religion's ancient holy days, the dates differ from one year to the next. The Chinese New Year can fall at any time from around the third week of January to the third week of February.

Some years ago, I discovered that those born right at the beginning of a new Chinese sign seem to have characteristics that are more akin to the previous sign, and it seems as though the sign that is passing away is reluctant to relinquish its influence. If you happen to be born in the early stages of a new Chinese animal sign, please read the information for the one that precedes yours in addition to the one to which you are supposed to belong. Some Chinese astrologers do suggest that you treat the first three or four weeks of a new sign as if it belonged to the previous one.

At one point, the ancient Chinese scholars threw out the old lunar method of setting the date for the New Year and used an "Imperial" date that translates in our western calendar to the fourth of February. Many systems of divination that rely upon dates take the fourth of February as the first day of a new year.

The ten stems and twelve branches

The basis of a great deal of Chinese philosophy, including Chinese astrology is to be found in the idea of the ten stems and twelve branches. The ten stems are supposedly heavenly in origin while the twelve branches are earthly. The ten stems are better known to us as the five elements, each of which has two different characters depending upon whether they are Active (Yang) or Receptive (Yin). The twelve branches are the familiar animal signs of the zodiac.

The ten celestial stems

The following list is called the Ganzhi system, and it shows one method of dividing up the elements into the ten stems. As always in Chinese divination, there are slight variations in names from one system to the next, depending upon the translator. The column marked element shows the basic element in the form that it appears in nature, while the column marked variation shows how that element is named for use in everyday life. The basic elements are Wood, Fire, Earth, Metal and Water.

Name	Yang/Yin	Element	Variation
Jia	Yang	Hard wood	Tree
Yi	Yin	Soft wood	Cut timber
Bing	Yang	Sun fire	Lightening
Ding	Yin	Kitchen fire	Burning incense
Wu	Yang	Mountain earth	Hills
Ji	Yin	Sand earth	Earthenware
Geng	Yang	Crude metal	Ore for processing
Xin	Yin	Refined metal	Utensils
Ren	Yang	Sea water	Salt water
Gui	Yin	Rain water	Fresh water

The twelve terrestrial branches

These are the familiar animal signs of the Chinese zodiac, along with their Chinese names.

Zi	Rat
Chou	Ox
Yin	Tiger
Mao	Rabbit
Chen	Dragon
Si	Snake
Wu	Horse
Wei	Goat
Shen	Monkey
You	Rooster
Xu	Dog
Hai	Pig

FOUR

Face Reading

*The shape of the face - the three zones - the skin -
the thirteen divisions - other facial areas*

Face reading has a long history, and the ancient Chinese scholars who developed a workable system have long been forgotten. It is known that the ancient Egyptians understood how to read faces, while in the 19th century Europeans took an interest in it. In the early 1900s, an American Judge called Edward Vincent Jones worked out the basis of face reading and instituted an organization called The Personality Foundation, in which he taught the subject. Judge Jones went on to teach others, and this unusual Foundation is still going strong today under the guidance of Paul Elsner.

The shape of the face

Even without any specialized knowledge, we routinely assess the personality of others by their faces, and we only have to read a description of a character in a novel to instinctively grasp the nature of the person the author is telling us about. The Chinese take this much further by dividing faces up into different types of shape. Even allowing for the differences in racial characteristics around the world, the system works well. Any distortion or irregularity in face shape detracts from the personality and is said to make the subject either unpleasant or unlucky. If a particular part of the face appears out of place or different from the rest, this area indicates potential problems.

The basic face shapes are square, triangular, round and oval, but these can be extended to make up a number of different combinations. We in the west aren't impressed by round faces, but to the Chinese a little roundness indicates a cheerful person who can communicate well, and make money.

The three zones

The Chinese call the forehead area down to the eyebrows heaven, and this is associated with the early years of one's life. The middle section of the face, from the eyebrows down to the base of the nose is called human, and this is associated with the middle years. The lower section, from the base of the nose down to the bottom of the face is termed earth, and this is concerned with old age.

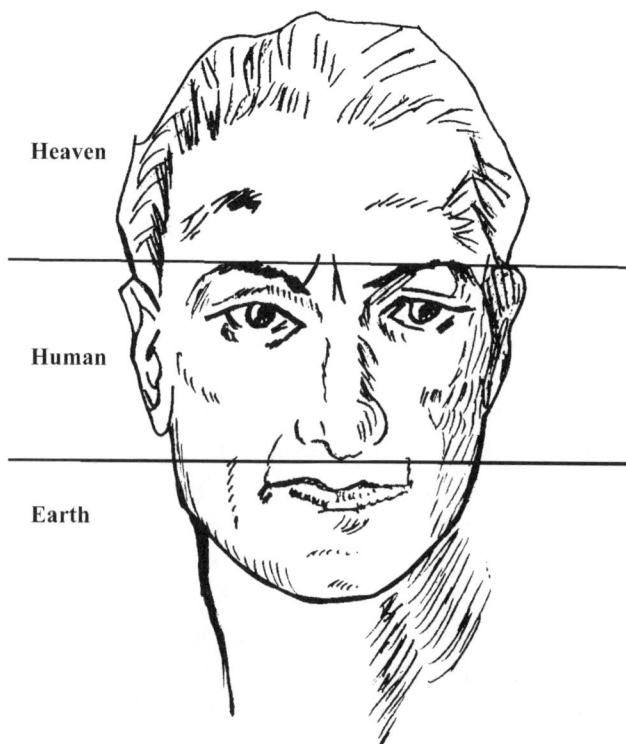

The three major areas of the face

An interesting connection...

There is an interesting co-relation here between the three zones used in handwriting analysis, because graphologists divide handwriting into three surprisingly similar zones. In graphology, the upper zone is associated with heavenly matters such as spirituality, intellect and philosophy, the middle one with human matters such as work, social life and one's behavior in a day-to-day sense, while the lower zone represents the earthy needs for financial security and sex.

Any part of the face that is scarred, malformed, dented or discolored suggests a problem with the aspect of the subject's life that is associated with that segment of his face. Grey or black marks, whether these are permanent features of the subject's face or just a temporary situation, denote problems that are themselves either temporary or permanent depending upon the type of mark. Even if nothing more than a trick of the light causes a mark, it will mean something.

Heaven

If the upper zone is well formed, clean, clear and well developed, the subject will have a good start in life and a useful education. Scarring, dents or discoloration here indicate a troubled childhood and a poor education. The problems will be worse for a man if the disfigurement is on the left and for a woman if it is on the right. A wide forehead is generally considered to be beneficial, but in a woman a very wide forehead suggests poor personal relationships. Those who take this subject further should also study the lines on the forehead as each of these has something to say. If you consider that the hair line represents the start of life and the eyebrows the end of absolute youth, say around the age of 21, any line or mark can easily be dated.

As you would imagine, a high forehead belongs to an intellectual personality, but the subject will be more creative and nicer to know if the forehead is broad. A high, narrow forehead belongs to a far more calculating and thrifty type of personality. An average forehead suggests a balanced personality that is bright, sensible, practical and kind-hearted. A low forehead belongs to a realistic person who may be clever with his hands, or he may have a strong and athletic body. A very low narrow forehead belongs to a stubborn, willful and possibly somewhat stupid type of person.

Human

If this section of the face is nicely balanced and if it fits comfortably with the rest of the face, the subject is likely to have a happy and productive life with stable relationships and a successful career. If this section is longer than the other two sections, the subject will be determined and self-disciplined. We will look more closely at this section of the face when we come to study the individual features.

Earth

If this section of the face is well formed and free from blemishes, the subject can expect a happy old age and good relationships with his children and grandchildren. He should live to a ripe old age with enough prosperity to make this comfortable. If this section is blemished or malformed, the outlook for a prosperous and happy old age is less favorable.

The skin

Before leaving the face in general, let us take a look at the skin type. Regardless of race or color, a fine skin belongs to a sensitive personality whose energy levels are quite low. A coarser skin-type belongs to a sturdy outdoorsman or to a tougher person who lacks sensitivity or intuition and who isn't tuned in to the moods of others.

The 13 divisions of the face

The Chinese further divide the face into 13 sub-sections. Here is a very simplified form of the 13-section reading, starting from the top of the face and working downwards.

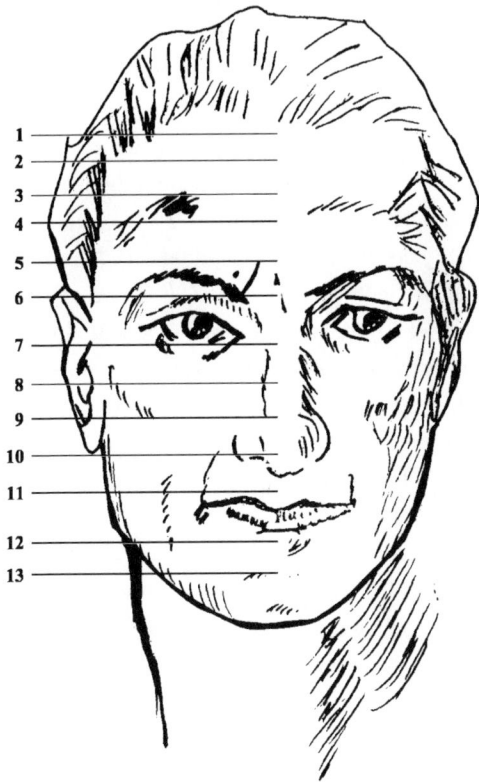

The 13 divisions of the face

1.   T'ien chung.

If this is clean and clear, the subject will have a happy childhood and youth and a good relationship with the parents. The subject's parents will live to a ripe old age. If it is marked or misshapen, there will be unhappiness during youth, and poverty or discord in the childhood home. Veins, dark marks and so forth here suggest accidents and sudden losses of money or prestige. A widow's peak suggests that the father may pass away before the mother.

2.   T'ien t'ing.

This is similar to the above, but it supplies information about the mother rather than the father. Negatively, a marked area suggests that the subject won't be believed when he is telling the truth.

3.   Ssu K'ung.

Much the same as the above. A good complexion here suggests a fortunate and successful life, while discolorations tell of a bad patch in the subject's career.

4.   Chung cheng.

If dented, the intellect will be low; if scarred, bumpy or sporting a mole, the subject will be impatient and unable to bring his plans to fruition, either as a result of bad public relations skills or bad luck. He will also find it hard to make and keep friends.

5.   Yin t'ang.

If this is healthy, the subject will receive an inheritance and will succeed in business. Eyebrows that meet or almost meet denote failure, bad luck and a lack of respect from other people. Marks, scars and black moles can indicate anything from adoption to illness and failure, and sometimes even a term of imprisonment! Wrinkles or creases between the eyebrows are considered to be of no consequence if the subject is over 40 years of age, otherwise they denote difficulties, tension and even a jealous nature.

6.   No Chinese name given.

Grayness here denotes illness, whereas a green patch at the side indicates possible adultery. A mole suggests stomach problems, emigration or imprisonment.

7.   Nien shang.

Moles here suggest stomach trouble, relationship problems or possibly an ill partner. Darkness here denotes a sick child.

8.   Shou shang.

A high bony nose suggests failure in business. Moles and discolorations signify a sick husband and difficulties with females.

9.   Chun t'ou.

The tip of the nose should be full in shape and clear of marks, hairs and blackheads for good fortune.

10.   Jen chung.

This is the grooved area between the base of the nose and the mouth. If the base of the groove is wider than the upper part, and the indentation neither too deep nor too flat, the subject will have healthy children and will achieve a high level of wealth and status in life. If it is wider at the top and shallow in shape, the subject will experience difficulties in having children, and his nature will be sour and ill mannered. Relationships will be difficult. If this area is bent, the subject will be childless and he will also be deceitful and unpopular. A straight line that is marked down the middle of the groove denotes children late in life. Also a wide area towards the top suggests happiness in early life, while width towards the bottom of the groove brings joy later in life.

11.   Shui hsing.

The mouth. This should be reasonably full with a pinkish color and upturned corners to ensure prosperity, good health and a happy marriage.

12.   Ch'eng chiang.

If this area is dark in the morning, the subject should avoid travelling over water during the course of that day. A man who has a hairless gap beneath his lower lip or a person of either sex who has a discoloration or a scar in this area must be careful of their diet, as the stomach may be weak.

13.   Ti ko.

This should be round, slightly protuberant and strong in appearance. A sharp chin is unlucky. If the chin points to the side, the subject will hold grudges against others. Any scarring or discoloration denotes money losses, possibly the loss of an inheritance. This can also foretell family illness and accidents.

The forehead

Strangely enough the shape of the forehead also follows the rules of graphology, because a high forehead suggests an intellectual or spiritual approach, while a medium one denotes a sensible, social and humane nature. A low forehead denotes a good intellect that might be put to willful or selfish ends, especially while seeking the basics of life such as money, food, material goods or sex. The area between the eyebrows should be a healthy color and free of marks for good health and vigor.

Eyes and eyebrows
Fine eyebrows are said to belong to a refined and intellectual person while the bushy type is seen on a more dominant and successful subject. Nobody seems to have time for people whose eyes are close together, and the Chinese consider this type to be greedy, suspicious, selfish and anxious. If the eyes are small, the subject is also secretive and evasive. The well-loved wide-eyed type is considered to be a good type of person and if the eyes are large, this subject is also very romantic. Eyebrows that are close to the eyes denote a shy, reticent person while those that are high on the face belong to a choosy, fussy subject. One piece of information that I have found is that people with what the Chinese call "Cat's Eyes", which are round with a yellowish glittering cast, have a magnetic personality, and that they love to be surrounded by beauty and to spend money on themselves. In my experience, such eyes are often found on people whose rising sign is Leo, and the description of their personality fits very well.

Noses
A strong nose belongs to a strong personality and if it is straight, the subject is both creative and practical as well as being honest. A hooked nose belongs on the face of a dynamic, ambitious, shrewd and astute business-person, while a ski-jump nose makes for a reasonable person with a happy nature and a good sense of humor. A flat and insignificant nose is said to belong to a person who lacks ambition.

Cheekbones
High cheekbones belong to an extrovert who will go far, while flat cheekbones denote a worrisome and insecure personality.

Ears

Round ears suggest artistic skills and good taste while pointed ones belong to a perceptive and intuitive type who doesn't take anything on trust. Rectangular ears denote honesty and fair play, while long ears belong to a more rigid personality. There is an old wives' tale that long ears denote a long life. It is true that old people do indeed tend to have long ears, but they may not have started out with them. Oddly enough, ears continue to grow throughout life, which is why older people's ears are inevitably long.

Lips

Obviously the best kind of mouth is one that is of medium size and evenly balanced, as this denotes emotional stability, refinement and a fair share of success in life. A thin top lip with a full lower lip is said to denote too great an interest in chasing the opposite sex and also an argumentative nature. If the lower lip protrudes, the person will never be satisfied with what he or she has in life, and may be easily taken in by unscrupulous people. A protruding top lip denotes an unkind person who doesn't know how to love. A small mouth denotes shyness and suspicion, while a large mouth suggests confidence. A turned up mouth suggests happiness and luck, while a badly formed mouth denotes sadness and financial loss. Lips that are set back in the face belong to an egotistic personality. The Chinese attach sexual indulgence to the person whose mouth is always slightly open. They may be right, but this person might also suffer from sinus problems!

The chin and jaw

As in films and comic books, the square chin belongs to the hero type, while a rounded chin belongs to a friendly personality, and a pointed chin suggests talent and a good imagination. A square jaw adds tolerance, while a rounded one can make the subject anxious and a small chin with jowls behind it denotes a timid and fearful personality who can suddenly lose his temper when he feels that he is being got at.

These days, much can be done to even out a "difficult" face. Bushy eyebrows that meet in the middle can be tweezed or treated by electrolysis, while moles, strawberries and coffee stains can be reomoved, and laser surgery or plastic surgery can treat even scars. A jaw or lips that are likely to be out of balance due to dental problems are routinely treated in childhood by orthodontics. A hooked nose, receding chin, sunken cheekbones or any other defect can be improved by plastic surgery. Whether this has any lasting effect upon a person's nature or their chances for luck in life is a moot point, but it makes sense that if a person is at ease with his or her face, they will be more confident.

Those of you would like to know more about this subject should look at the further reading list at the back of this book.

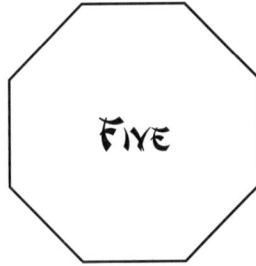

FIVE

Feng Shui

Approaching the subject - pronunciation - what is Feng Shui? - siting a property - the frontage - front door - back door - hallway - windows - beams & secret arrows - living room - dining area - kitchen - studies & workrooms - bedroom - child's room - bathroom & toilet - single living space - the Magic Square - Yang & Yin - the elements - lucky numbers - public restrooms

How I have approached this subject

I have opened this chapter by taking a look at the site the house is on, moving to the house as a whole and finally looking at the best arrangement for each room. I show how problem rooms can be improved by using colors, mirrors, ornaments, plants and so on. The final part of this chapter shows how you can find your own personal direction and room arrangement by means of the Feng Shui magic square system. I haven't gone into the use of Feng Shui in business except in the most general terms, but many of the general principles that apply to household Feng Shui can be adapted to a working environment.

Pronunciation

People pronounce Feng Shui in a variety of ways, not least in China itself, so however you care to say these words will be right somewhere. The word for the strange unseen energy that Feng Shui experts talk about is usually spelled Chi, but it is sometimes spelled Qi or Ki, as in Nine Star Ki. If you want to be strictly correct, pronounce this word Kee; if, like me, you are used to the Chi spelling and pronounce it the way it looks, that's fine. Incidentally, having lived and worked in South China, I use their pronunciation for Feng Shui, which is roughly " Fung Shoy".

What is Feng Shui?

Feng Shui is the art of placement, which is a way of balancing all the elements, in order to create harmony within a locality or a building. The background to the system derives from a number of ideas, some of which are very complicated, and these are added to normal human feelings of safety, danger and plain straightforward common sense. People like it and it seems to have worked wonders for the Chinese, so let us not poke holes in the system, but use it wisely so that it can work for us.

Long ago, and long before Feng Shui became fashionable in the west, an old China hand told me that the Chinese believe that bad spirits travel in straight lines and good ones travel in wavy lines. This man also said that a straight path that leads directly to the front door is simply asking for bad spirits to zoom in. If you have such a path and can do nothing to change it, at least put a gate at the end of it and break up the straight line with a couple of tubs of plants or with plants that tumble over the edges of the path.

A deeper look into the Feng Shui system showed me that this spiritual energy is called Chi, and this can be negative or positive depending upon its flow. Chi is said to be negative if it is encouraged to flow too quickly, too slowly or to stagnate, while positive Chi flows along and swirls around gently. If you think of Chi as actual air moving around, it will be easier to understand the principles that follow in this chapter. In addition to getting the Chi energies right, there is a natural human need to feel safe and protected, to have something solid at one's back and to be able to see what is coming towards one. Feng Shui takes all these ideas into consideration.

A few minor reservations

Every Feng Shui source that I have come across insists that clutter should be cleared away, that cupboards and wardrobes should be shut, and that all those bits and pieces that we accumulate be kept from view. I am not too sure about this. Many times in my life I have seen businesses prosper in small, cluttered and scruffy environments while beautiful places fold. I have seen happy people living untidily and less happy ones in pristine surroundings. Too much clutter is confusing, too much tidiness is uncomfortable, so I guess the middle way is probably best.

A slightly worrying aspect of the system is that there are different schools of thought giving conflicting advice, so in this book, I will stick to the kind of basics with which few practitioners could disagree. Another consideration is to keep within the bounds of reason and not to be silly when applying Feng Shui. Two stories from China itself demonstrate what I mean by this. One man was advised to drive his car up the steps towards his house, as this would take him "up the stairway to promotion". The promotion was not forthcoming and his car suffered from driving up and down steps. Another man was advised to sleep with a mirror beneath his pillow, to improve his intelligence. The mirror trick may have worked if it was only a tiny one, but this man used a large mirror and ended up with a very stiff neck in addition to remaining stupid.

Finally, an evil or immoral person won't have good luck in the long run, whatever he does.

Siting a house or place of business

If it is possible to choose your home or workplace, try to ensure that the front of the building, and in particular the front entrance, is not facing rising ground and that you can see clearly from the front of your house. The idea here is much the same as for a

Saxon stronghold, i.e. that you should be able to see everything that is coming towards you.

In a hilly area, you should ensure that the front entrance faces a downhill slope or flat land. If there is a pond or a meandering stream somewhere in front of the house, so much the better. If the stream or river flows too quickly, or from left to right, or if it is at an angle to the property, that is bad news. If it flows from right to left and meanders gently, that is fine. This ensures that the house is protected at the back and that the front catches good Chi "breath" or pleasant breezes. Avoid living with running water at the back of your property.

Another Chinese story that I have come across concerns a wealthy Hong Kong businessman who built a lovely home for himself and his family on one of Hong Kong's many islands. The house was correctly sited with a hill at the back and the sea in front. The rooms were perfectly proportioned and everything else was fine. However, this man's luck ran out from the moment that he and his family moved into the house. The family was beset by illness and loss and his business began to fail, so in desperation, the businessman called in a Feng Shui expert. The expert could find nothing wrong, but he asked if he could live in the house for a while to see if there was anything that he might have missed. One day, the expert gazed idly out of the window at the sea at the ebbing tide and suddenly he noticed a large rock emerging from the water. This rock looked for all the world like a great ugly toad with its mouth open - and it's devouring jaws were pointed right at the house! The expert told the businessman to move himself and his family out of the house forthwith. The businessman promptly moved, abandoning the house, which then stood empty for many years. This cost him money in the short term, but his luck improved immediately the family's health improved, and he soon regained his wealth.

Not too many people live by rivers or the seaside, but many millions live alongside roads. Feng Shui suggests that you treat all roads as if they were rivers. A front door that faces a "T" junction with traffic coming straight towards it is not good, especially if this is a one-way road with all the traffic flowing straight at property before turning away. This is tolerable when the entrance to the building is at the side of the property, as the traffic flow won't appear to be directed into the "mouth" of the house. As with the river, you should try to avoid living with a busy main road behind your property.

Jan and I were recently taken for a meal at Nando's restaurant in Earls Court. The lady who entertained us was the daughter of the owner of the Nando chain of restaurants and she is very into Feng Shui. She told us that when this particular restaurant was opened, it did very poor business despite being in a prime area, close to Earls Court tube station. Her father called in a Feng Shui expert who looked the place over. The restaurant is on a "T" junction, but this shouldn't have caused any problems because it is a one-way street with the traffic moving away from the restaurant rather than towards it. However, high up on a building on the corner of the junction were two black stone statues of devils that were pointing their forefingers right at the restaurant. The owners had a curved brass plaque made, somewhat in the shape of an ancient Greek soldier's shield, which they attached to the wall beside the restaurant window facing directly towards the devils - and bingo, business started to boom!

The Chinese try to avoid living in houses whose front entrances and courtyards face north, as these catch the wind and yellow dust from the Mongolian plains. Western homes encourage people to live at the back of the house and to spend time in the kitchen and the garden, so for us a north-facing frontage might be preferable, with the sunny south around the back. Southern hemisphere homes can face south and have the sun at the back of the house.

You must try to avoid living or working in a place that overlooks a graveyard or a funeral parlor, because this reminds you of your own mortality and it is considered to be very unlucky. Gargoyles, nasty looking animal statues or anything else of a hostile nature that point towards the house should be avoided.

Directly in front of the house

A straight path or driveway that ends at the front door will direct unlucky spirits and too much fast moving Chi right to your door. A curved driveway or one that goes around something is best. A wide path is better than a narrow one, and it shouldn't go around a sharp corner before arriving at the house. If you only have room for a straight narrow path, then break this up with a tub or two of plants.

An anatomy of a house

A square shaped house is best, but if you are in the UK, it is likely that your house has a narrow frontage and is deeply rectangular, so you will have to treat each part of the house as a separate entity. Try to ascertain the position of the center of your premises, because this is the area that relates to health. Keep this area clear and tidy if you want to stay well.

The front door

One of the main areas of interest to a Feng Shui expert is the front door, because this is called the "mouth" of the house and it is considered to be the place where good or evil can pour in. Apart from the considerations that we have already covered, such as roads, rivers etc. the door should not face anything that will shoot what the Chinese call secret arrows at it. Secret arrows need not be as dramatic as the two black devil statues that feature in the Nando's restaurant story, but there may be something as ordinary as a lamp-post, a high fence, a satellite dish, a telephone pole or a sharp corner facing the front of the house.

You can't have a lamp-post moved and you can't ask your neighbor opposite to tear down his garden wall, but you can put a brass plaque or even a large brass doorknob on the door to deflect and reflect the arrows away. One very easy solution is to fix a Pa Kua mirror to the front door, either on the outside of the door or inside if there is a bit of glass at the top, or in a window adjacent to the door. The Pa Kua mirror must face outwards, of course. Also a solid wooden door is better than a glass one, as that gives more Feng Shui protection and it is also less likely to be broken into. Another good idea is to hang a picture of a tiger in your hall, facing the front door, as this will help to dispel bad influences. You can paint the front door an auspicious color, or if all else fails you can brick up the doorway and use another entrance to your house. We look at colors, shapes and elements later in this part of the book.

The back door

This is not as important as the front door, but it can be used to encourage good Chi into the house. While a glass front door is frowned upon, a glass pane in the back door is considered to be beneficial. It is best for the door to face an open area rather than a blank wall, as this will encourage good Chi to enter the house at the back. If your door does face a blank wall, perhaps you could ask someone to paint a mural on it, or you could hang some plants or some Spanish style colored china or terracotta ornaments on it, to brighten it up.

The hallway

The worst case scenario is a dead straight hallway that shoots from the front door to the back of the house with nothing to obstruct its path. Imagine the kind of wind tunnel that is used to test out the aerodynamics of an airplane. If the wind tunnel were to operate without a plane inside it, the wind would simply shoot through in a straight line. In such a hallway, the Chi shoots through so quickly that it doesn't stop anywhere long enough to do any good.

If you can't tear down your house in order to alter the shape of such a hallway, at least put something in it that will force the flow of Chi to slow down and to bend and sway. A semicircular occasional table against the wall would help, as would an old fashioned hat and coat stand, a chair, an umbrella stand or anything else that you have room for. If the hall is so narrow that there is nothing you can put in it, then hang a few plaques, plates, pictures with raised surfaces or mirrors with prominent frames on the wall to break up the wind-tunnel effect. If you can put mats down in such a way that they are safe, choose oval ones with a curvy pattern on them. The worst case is where the front and back doors are in alignment. If this is the case, hang some Chimes or some light fittings with fancy shades from the hall ceiling close by the front and back doors in order to break up the Chi movement.

One idea that would appear totally crazy to the western mind is to buy a toy flute or penny whistle and attach this to the wall above the front and back doors. The reason for this is that the Chinese word for flute is close to their word for disappear, and this will encourage any bad spirits to disappear from your house. I guess it's worth a try, although it may be more effective in a Chinese environment.

If the hallway is gloomy, paint it a pale color and put some decent lighting in it. If your staircase rises directly upwards and especially if it faces your front door, lay a mat with a curvy shape or pattern on the floor. This will encourage the Chi energy to flow around softly.

Windows

All windows should open out on to some kind of view and not on to a blank wall or high hedge. This harks back to less law abiding days when houses needed to be made as safe as possible. From this point of view, even today it is worth ensuring that a vulnerable window is lockable or to fit one of those Spanish style wrought iron guards over it.

This may seem more like common sense than Feng Shui, and the following advice follows in the same vein. Windows should open to encourage cool breezes in hot weather, but they should be shaded with blinds or curtains when the sun is too strong. Better still, they should close properly in bad weather. If you can't afford double-glazing, good, thick, lined curtains are a good old-fashioned substitute during the worst of the winter.

Beams and secret arrows

The Chinese don't like exposed ceiling beams, especially over the dining table or the bed. If you have such a beam and there is nothing that you can do about it, hang a small dangling ornament or Chime from it to break up its oppressive effect. The same goes for attic rooms with steeply sloping roofs. If you have to sleep in such a room, paint curvy patterns on the sloping ceiling, attach colored posters or hang up chimes, mobile ornaments or interesting light fittings.

If any sharp corners or the edges of wardrobes, cupboards and appliances point to where a member of the family sits, eats or sleeps, try putting a mirror on the wall facing it so that the secret arrows thrown out by the corner are reflected back. Another solution would be to soften the edge or corner by covering it with a piece of material.

The living room

A nice square or rectangular living room is best, as there is nowhere for Chi to collect and stagnate. If you do have an odd shaped corner or a "leg" off your room, hang up a Chime, put a plant on a table or a stand there, to help the Chi to start moving around once again. The center of any room is the health area and this should be kept clear.

There are differing views about how you arrange your seating, with some experts saying that your seats could be close to the walls and others saying they should be away from the walls. In reality, your arrangement will often be dictated by the size of your room. If you can avoid putting a seat either with its back immediately in front of a window or directly facing a window, then do so. The idea here is that it is unsafe to have things going on behind you or to be facing into the glare of the sun. Once again, this harks back to days when bandits or other enemies might attack the home.

If possible, furniture should be in keeping with the size of the room. Avoid placing chairs under exposed beams as this will make the person sitting in them uneasy or oppressed. Most people put flowers and plants in their living rooms; this encourages good Chi and softens any secret arrows that may be present. The Chinese prefer pot plants to cut flowers, as they are alive and growing rather than dying in the vase, but if you like cut flowers (as I do), ensure that you throw them out before they die off. Dried flowers are symbolic of death, so they are not liked. Oddly enough, the Chinese dislike mirrors over the fireplace as this encourages Chi to fly up the chimney! If the fireplace is ornamental rather than functional, a mirror won't be a problem. As a living room is Yang by nature, a few soft cushions and a touch of green or blue will help to balance it.

The dining area

The dining table should be circular, or at least have no hard-edged corners, and it should be under a good light so that the diners can see what they are eating. Use plain wall colorings rather than busy ones in this area, because nothing should distract the diners from their food or upset their digestion. The Chinese are like continental Europeans in that they prefer to eat sitting around a table, talking and enjoying the meal, so they would take a dim view of the modern habit of eating on one's lap while watching television.

An odd number of chairs suggests that someone in the family is lonely. Naturally, there will be occasions when you have an odd number of people at your table, but you should have a spare chair somewhere around. Chairs with arms are said to be luckier than ones without arms. If possible, try to avoid placing diners with their backs to a window, and try not to sit with your own back to a door. Chairs with rounded arms are preferable. In a living/dining room, it is best to separate the eating area from the rest of the room with a screen or some plants in tubs.

The kitchen

The Chinese take cooking and eating very seriously and they consider the kitchen to be the most important room in the house. If a bathroom adjoins the kitchen, a double door should separate the toilet area from it. If this is impossible, install one of those plastic folding doors to shut the toilet away. The kitchen should also be clean, clear of unnecessary clutter, well lit and well ventilated.

Kitchen Feng Shui is practical in that it suggests that appliances and equipment that come under the rulership of fire and water should be separated. Therefore, the cooker should not be sited adjacent to either the sink or the fridge. The oven should be in a well lit and ventilated area and it should face sideways on to the front and back doors. The same goes for the main work surface, as the cook should not have his or her back to a door. This follows the rules of never being in a position where an enemy can creep up and attack the cook. If it is not possible to place the working surface or oven in this way, hanging a mirror above will help. The oven or stove shouldn't be directly beneath a skylight, as this will dissipate the good Chi. A clean stovetop will ensure that your money luck increases. A very small and practical kitchen will be almost entirely composed of the elements of fire and water, so introduction of the wood element will help to balance this. Wooden cupboard fronts, a wooden bread-bin and utensils, and introducing the color green in the decor or kitchen knickknacks will do the trick. Cutlery should not be put into a corner drawer, as this "dead" area is filled with stagnant Chi.

Studies and workrooms

If you have a study, a studio or a place where younger members of the family do their homework, the usual recommendation of curved furniture is reversed. Curves encourage slow-moving and relaxing Chi, but in a room where sharpness of the mind is required, square shapes are best. Therefore, tables, cupboards, shelves etc. should be square. If a corner shoots a particularly nasty secret arrow towards the person doing the studying, placing a mirror or a shiny ornament on an opposing wall or shelf will shoot it back again. A desk should not face a window because the glare will upset you when you work at it. Never work with your back to a door, as this will make you feel insecure.

If only part of a room is used for paperwork or study, use pot plants or a screen to divide this area from the rest of the room. This is particularly important in a bedroom because a good night's sleep is needed. Try not to have a computer screen directly facing the foot of a bed. Work areas are notorious for collecting clutter and mess, so try to keep your workspace in some semblance of order, and use boxes and cupboards to keep as much as possible out of sight.

The bedroom

We spend a third of our lives asleep and we need peace at night if we are to function properly during the day. Feng Shui principles ensure a sense of well being and harmony that induces rest and a good night's sleep. I read somewhere recently that somebody has proved that good sleeping patterns enhance the memory... but I can't remember where I saw that! The bed is associated with sex and by extension with marriage, so a good bedroom layout is essential if you want a happy marriage and a halfway decent sex life.

A bedroom should be upstairs or off the sitting area, and it should only have one entrance so that the Chi circulates in the room rather than passing through it. You shouldn't sleep with your head or your feet directly facing the door. The idea is that with your head towards the door you can't see who is coming into the room. I was brought up with the Jewish superstition that one shouldn't sleep with one's feet directly opposite a door because dead bodies are taken out of a room feet first. While looking into the principles of Feng Shui, I discovered that the Chinese believe the same thing for the same reason.

An en-suite bathroom is said to draw energy from the sleeper if his feet face directly towards the door. A skylight above the bed or your feet facing directly opposite a window will have the same effect. In an attic room, it is best to sleep with your head away from the constricted area where the ceiling slopes and in any kind of bedroom an overhead beam over the bed will cause sleeplessness and depression. The same goes for a heavy light fitting or chandelier dangling over the bed.

Electricity is strongly Yang, so television sets, radios and computers should be kept out of the bedroom if possible. If you must have them, don't place them directly opposite the foot of the bed, and screen them from the bed during the night. The Chinese disapprove of electric blankets due to their Yang influence, but if you do use one, turn it off when you get into bed at night.

One real no-no is to have a mirror at the foot of the bed, or indeed anywhere close to the bed, because the Chinese believe that the soul leaves the body and goes on astral journeys while we sleep. If the returning soul sees its reflection in a mirror, it is said to take fright and fail to return to the sleeper's body. A dressing table mirror should not oppose the window, as the glare from outside will be reflected in it. Furniture should not be placed around the bed in an arc, as this will lower the health and vitality of the sleeper. Metal bedsteads can shoot "secret arrows" at a sleeper, so they should be avoided. The same goes for four poster beds. However, exposed beams and bars can be draped in material that softens their outline.

When choosing bedroom furniture, tread a fine line between very angular lines and abrupt corners that shoot "secret arrows", and totally rounded shapes that encourage the Chi to move around too quickly. Square furniture with rounded corners would probably be best.

A child's room

A child's bedroom should be in the southeastern sector of the house. This should be changed to the northeastern sector for those who live in the Southern Hemisphere. This will encourage the life-giving energy of the rising sun to enter the room and benefit the health of the child.

A rectangular room with adequate ventilation and light is best, and common sense suggests that it be close to the parent's room. A mobile close to the window will encourage the Chi to move about gently. If you have a choice of color for your child's room, choose pale green, as this is associated with the east and the rising sun. A very active child can be calmed down by introducing some blue into the room, while a shy and submissive one should have a bit of red around in order to encourage self-confidence.

The bathroom and toilet suite

The best direction for a bathroom is usually to the north, as this aligns with the water element. Water colors are black and dark blue, so these could be introduced by using the odd bit of ornamentation or decoration on the occasional wall tile, or by choosing towels in those colors. If you want to balance your bathroom with a bit of the fire element, use pink shades. A wooden loo seat introduces a touch of the wood element into the bathroom and it will help to balance the energies.

Keep bathroom doors closed if you don't want your money to fall down the toilet. If it is possible to train your family to keep the toilet lid down, do so. The center of the house is considered the most important because this is the health area, so a toilet should never face into this part of the house. Wherever your toilet is, placing a small round mirror on the inside of the door to reflect the effect back inside can minimize its draining effect. Alternately, a small round mirror can be placed on the outside of the door to reflect the good Chi from the hallway or any facing rooms back on to themselves. The bathroom or toilet door should never face the bedroom door, as this will mess up your love relationship in no time at all.

Ensure that taps don't drip and that everything in your bathroom functions properly. A leaky tap or cistern ensures that your friends will lean heavily on you and they may also drain you of financial resources. It is best to have some form of natural light in a bathroom, but if it is entirely windowless, mirrors will help prevent stagnant Chi from building up. Living plants are another aid to encouraging the gentle movement of beneficial Chi. As this room is so Yin in nature, it might be an idea to introduce a little Yang by placing a few candles in it. Some of those lovely crystal stones that gift shops sell are also a good idea. A ventilation device will drag good Chi from a bathroom or a toilet, so decorate it with something colorful or attach a small wind-chime to it.

A single living space

If all you have is what we British call a bedsit and Americans sometimes call an efficiency, the best approach is to find some way of differentiating between working, living and sleeping areas. As always, try to keep a clear space in the middle of the room in order to promote good health. If the room is an odd shape, use a cut off corner for your sleeping area. If you can't do much about the room, at least separate your working and sleeping areas as much as you can and avoid boxing in your sleeping area with furniture.

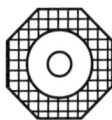

The Feng Shui Magic Square

This is where things get a little more technical, but there is nothing difficult about this for you to take on board, so read through this section and see how you can use the information to enhance your life.

At various points in this book, you will find the same concepts coming into use in a variety of ways, and Feng Shui is no exception to this. The first is the balance of the active Yang force and the receptive or passive Yin force. Another important factor is that of the five elements and the directions that they relate to. Feng Shui experts would also include the numerology systems that appear in the chapter on the Lo Shu.

Yang and Yin

The list below covers some of the concepts that come under the auspices of Yang and Yin. If you use a little imagination, this will give you some idea about how to balance the rooms in your house, how to improve your work area, or even your car. For instance, a few heavy ornaments, table lamps or vases will introduce a little Yin into the mainly Yang nature of a living room. In a Yin area such as a bathroom, a couple of solid, light-colored ornaments or a pale rug will help to introduce some Yang. The table below will give you a clue as to the kind of rugs, ornaments, objects and colors that you can introduce to swing the balance one way or another.

Yang	Yin
Male	Female
Light	Dark
Hot	Cold
Hard	Soft
Light	Heavy
Fire	Water
Sharp	Blunt
Right	Left
Up	Down
Front	Back

Solid   Empty
Angular   Curved
Moving   Static

The five elements

The elements have already appeared in the astrology chapter of this book, but to refresh your memory, these are Wood, Fire, Earth, Metal and Water. Each element helps the next one in turn when the cycle is kept in this order.

Wood fuels Fire

Fire creates Earth (ashes)

Earth creates Metal

Metal can flow like Water

Water feeds Wood

Harking back to the chapter on astrology, you may remember that the elements that are next to each other are harmonious to each other, while those that are two apart are inharmonious. The classic clash is between Fire and Water, which is why Feng Shui suggests that you should not have a stove and a sink adjacent to each other. Elements can be added to break up a destructive pattern. An example of this is the advice given in the kitchen section about adding something of the Wood element to the Fire and Water area of the house. Wood is compatible with both Water and Fire.

Each element is associated with a color and a shape. This means that a rug, ornament, light fitting, candles or cushions can be added in a compatible color or shape in order to create a balance. For instance, to inject some life into your bedroom and into your love life, try placing red, white or pink (red plus white) candles or ornaments in the room. If you only want a peaceful night's sleep, blue is the color. You might place something from the element of Earth in your work area. Such an object could be a square rug - especially if it was predominantly yellow - or you could have a plant in a yellow earthenware pot. A few crystals of any color, or polished stones around the place will have the same effect. For a peaceful sitting room, hang up blue or green curtains or use blue or green cushions. In a disco or in an area that you use for sports, use some white, silver and red. Shapes can be added as per the table below.

Element	Color	Shape
Water	black, dark blue	wavy lines
Wood	Green	Rectangle
Fire	Red	Triangle
Earth	Yellow	Square
Metal	White, silver	circle, oval

Introduce a few living plants into an office, hospital or factory, especially if it is full of metal objects. You can calm a busy area down or relieve a place that has too much fiery pink and red with a tank of fish. If you want to brighten up a blue/green place and introduce some life into it, use red, pink and orange ones candles. A few crystals or a china pot can enliven a room that is too soft and fluffy. If you want to shift a stagnant blocked-off corner of the room, use the Metal element in chimes, a picture frame or a piece of statuary. Place a mirror on the wall that faces a window that opens onto a nice view because this will draw whatever is outside into the room.

The Magic Square

The Magic Square or Lo Shu is behind a great many of the Chinese divinations. Its origins are covered more fully in the history chapter earlier in this book. The Magic Square is a grid of small Squares containing the numbers 1 to 9, arranged so that whichever way they are added up - horizontally, vertically or diagonally - they always add up to 15.

4	9	2
3	5	7
8	1	6

Magic Square

The Feng Shui numerology associated with the numbers in the Magic Square is as follows:

1. Career prospects, your self-esteem. Your potential in business and the role you play in society.
2. Relationships of all kinds, especially marriage, partnerships and romance.
3. The past, your ancestors and your original home. This may not mean much to Westerners, but the Chinese respect the past and they often invoke spiritual help from their ancestors when times are rough. This area also relates to family relationships with parents, grandparents, other older relatives and the prospect of inheritance.
4. The chances of gaining and keeping wealth.
5. Physical health and well being.
6. This is the area where the gods and spirits are called in to help you. Friends and allies can be attracted if this area is attractive. Travel is marked here and business travel is enhanced if this area is well treated.
7. Children, fertility and creation. This also governs creative gifts, creative hobbies and productive use of leisure time.
8. Education, knowledge and openness to new ideas. This brings new ideas into your life and if you need to spend time thinking, this is the place to do it.
9. Fame, reputation and recognition. On a more mundane level, this rules the way you are viewed or esteemed by others and the amount of respect that you win.

The most basic view of the Magic Square

4 - Prosperity	9 - Recognition	2 - Relationships
3 - Parents, etc.	5 - Health	7 - Children
8 - Study	1 - Career	6 - Friends

At this point, you can either visualize each floor of your home or workplace, or you can draw a plan of it. Place the Magic Square over your plan and put the front door at the front (bottom) of the Magic Square. If you normally use a door that is at the side of the house, put that side of the house at the front of the Square. If it is at a corner (as in some business premises), place the front of the Square at the front elevation of the building; imagine the view that people approaching the building see, and put the front of the Square there. I have repeated the Magic Square design below in order to help you. Don't forget to look back at the list to check out the meaning of each numbered square. If your house is an irregular shape, leave a part of the Magic Square unoccupied.

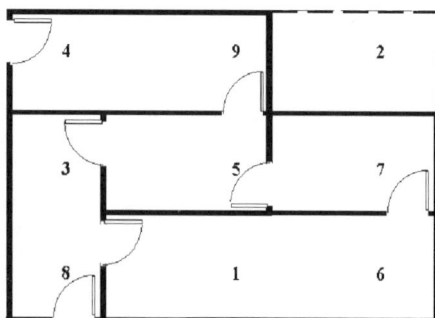

Front Door

```
| 4 | 9 | 2 |
| 3 | 5 | 7 |
| 8 | 1 | 6 |
```
Magic Square

Draw or visualize two diagonal lines from corner to opposite corner of your house or your place of work, and take note of where they cross. This will be the middle of the premises, and as this is the health area, it should be free of dirt and clutter. If a toilet occupies this position, you or the other occupants will become ill.

Every source that I have investigated while researching this book says that clutter and mess will affect your home and thus by extension your life, but who can expect to live in a show house or to work in a totally tidy environment? Having said this, real mess is disorientating and it can also be exhausting. While writing this book, Jan and I have moved house and we seem to have been living in some form of disorganization for weeks on end, so I can only agree that a disorganized home or workplace is very frustrating and tiring. So, I guess the answer here is to take a middle road and neither live in a show house or a junkyard.

1. **Career prospects:** Improve your career prospects by keeping this area neat and tidy. If your hallway is long and narrow, break up the swift-moving Chi by hanging some chimes up or by placing a semicircular table at the side. A picture of an animal facing the front door or an ornament of an animal placed so that it can look out of a window will help bring in good Chi and keep the bad stuff out. Anything made of Metal will help your career prospects, so a metal framed picture or mirror or a metal object would be worth placing close by the front door.

2.   **Relationships:** Put a picture of your partner in this area. Keep this area calm and attractive by adding pleasant colors and living plants.

3.   **Ancestors and family:** A picture of your parents, grandparents, in-laws or other relatives will aid your current relationship, and a picture of one who has passed on will help invoke his or her help from beyond the grave. If you have a bad relationship with your parents or in-laws, this might actually help.

4.   **Prosperity:** Hang a few of those Chinese coins that you can buy in tourist shops here. If you can't find any of these, put three, six or nine coins on a shelf or in the corner closest to the outside of the house. Water will help the flow of communications, so put some here if you want to communicate with others.

5.   **Health and strength:** Even if other areas of your home are untidy, try to keep this area clear and avoid placing anything dirty here. Dirty cups, ashtrays and so on should not be allowed to sit around in this area.

6.   **The gods, religion, friends, helpers and travel:** Pictures of your friends or of places you would like to visit can be hung here. If you like religious statuettes or pictures (any religion or spirituality), place them here.

7.   **Children, creativity:** A nice ornament here will help. If you want to be productive, something related to the element of Fire such as a red candle will help.

8.   **Study, contemplation:** Books are the obvious things to keep here, also magazines, perhaps also the television.

9.   **Recognition, esteem:** Buy an Oscar statuette from a gift shop and place it here. If there is any other symbol associated with your search for fame or status, put it here.

Having done this for your house as a whole, now go over each room with the Magic square and if something is out of kilter in your life, put something appropriate and optimistic in the representative room. For instance, if you work from home, place some coins in the money area of your workroom, or if you are looking for love, place a romantic picture there.

Finally, if your home is an irregular shape with an area of the Magic Square that falls outside your house, put a mirror on the wall with its back to the missing area, as this will bring the missing part into play.

Your lucky number

You might feel happier in a house with a particularly lucky number.

To find your own personal lucky number, add together the last two digits of the year of your birth. For example, if you were born in 1976, you would simply add 7 and 6.

If you happen to have been born between January 1 and February 3 (inclusive), you count your year as the previous one. For example, if you were born on January 17, 1967, you need to count your year as 1966.

Using the example of a person who was born in 1976, add 7 + 6 to make 13. If the number you arrive at is higher than nine, add the numbers together: 1 + 3 = 4.

Now we treat the sexes differently from each other. This derives from an ancient idea about Yang and Yin. Therefore, if the person is male, take the number 10 and subtract the year number from it. In our 1976 example this would be: 10 - 4 = 6.

If the person is female, add 5 to the year number, so for our example this would be: 4 + 5 = 9. If you end up with a number that is higher than 9, simply add the numbers together to reduce them.

If you can't live in a house with a number that is lucky for most members of the family, then at least do what you can to improve the Feng Shui inside the house.

The Lucky number can be used to assess the right direction for your house to face, but there are two problems with this. Firstly, there are so many conflicting Feng Shui ideas at work here that it is difficult to give you a definitive answer as to what is right. Secondly, the direction that might be lucky for you might not be for other members of your household. If you are not happy with the way your house faces, then place a Pa Kua mirror in the front window to dispel any bad Chi.

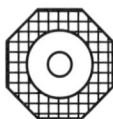

Chinese public restrooms

Despite the fact that the following has absolutely nothing to do with this book, I simply have to tell you something about Chinese public lavatories (rest rooms for American readers). China has never been overrun or colonized by western countries, so the Chinese do things their own way, which is quite different to the way things are done anywhere else. Unusually for a third world country, China is not filled with poverty stricken shacks and filth, and Chinese public restrooms are very clean, but they are also something to behold.

Some years ago when I was still married to my late husband, Tony Fenton, we took a tour around Guangzhu (Canton), and part of the trip took us on a visit to the zoo. After wandering around there for a while, I realized that I needed the bathroom, and this side trip turned out to be far more interesting than the sad sight of large animals in small cages. The inside of this loo was covered in mosaic, in shades of blue and white, and the whole thing was spotlessly clean. The doorway was wide and completely open, and being China, there was a large family group standing around by the doorway with a clear view of everything that was going on inside. Inside the building there were four areas for use, each divided by a waist high wall. I stepped into one to discover something that looked like a miniature canal with a "bank" on either side and a slot about a foot wide in the middle. This slot or ditch was about four feet deep and running through the bottom of it was a river of clean flowing water. There was no toilet paper, or indeed any kind of attachment for such a thing. Being a seasoned traveler, I always carry tissues in my pocket for just such contingencies, and I simply chucked my used tissue into the "river" and watched fascinated as it flowed away. Talk about fast moving Chi - nothing had a chance to stagnate there! There were sinks for hand washing and some paper towels and a wastebasket.

Later on the same trip, Tony rushed into a loo that was close by a railway station. Along the wall was a row of urinals, and the only unusual fact was that they were very low, rather like those in a school for small boys. The Chinese are smaller than western people, so I guess that the urinals needed to be lower. Tony was so absorbed by the need to concentrate on aiming into the contraption that for a while he failed to notice much else. Just before he was finished, he became aware of a slight commotion going on towards his left. As he turned to look, he saw that the left hand wall of the room was made of plate glass, and it looked straight out on to the street - for all the world like a shop window! By this time a sizeable crowd of Chinese had gathered to see how the tall gwailo (foreign devil) was getting on. He finished what he had to do, gave the crowd a wave, washed his hands and walked out of the loo with tears of laughter pouring down his face.

Some Feng Shui books go on about how the Chinese value privacy for their ablutions, but in my experience, the writers can't have actually visited China! City life, at least, is quite a different model...

Finally, I felt I had to include the following alternate view of
the Magic Square, which I came across while researching this book.
It is obviously a very ancient concept, and so far, I have not been
able to identify the meaning of such rich terminology as "The Mali-
cious Death position of the Five Yellow Curses". I am naturally
intrigued, and if I do find the meanings of some of the concepts
shown, I will certainly include them in future editions of this book.

NORTH

N/W			N/E
The position of the Three Jadeite Stars of Conflict	The Three Curses	The Malicious Death position of the Five Yellow Curses	
WEST Bloodshed	The Curse of Sickness	Peach Blossom	**EAST**
Primary Wealth promotion	Speculative income	Learning/ Wealth accumulation	
S/W			S/E

SOUTH

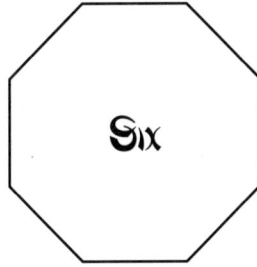

Six

Chinese Hand Reading

Methods - characteristics - links - hand areas - interpretations

Hand reading methods

There are many ways of reading hands and all of them are valid. In the west there are scientific hand readers who read the evidence that is seen on the hand, but we also come across psychic hand readers who use the hand as a means of tuning in psychically. There are plenty of scientific readers who bring in a certain amount of psychic ability, and plenty of psychics who know something about the lines and marks on the hand. Even among scientific palmists, there are variations in their methods, partly due to where they learned their craft in the first place and also due to what they pick up by experience along the way. China is a big country and it has a long history, so it is not surprising that there are a variety of methods in use. The ones in this book are a result of my research, but there must be plenty of other methods in use all over China.

Hand characteristics

The Chinese categorize the different types of hands by the elements, so that the a "knotted" hand is considered a Fire hand, while a smooth-fingered one is a Wood hand. The Water hand is far more rounded and it suggests that the person likes to travel and to talk. The Earth hand, with its square shape and square fingers, represents the same thing in any culture, which is a practical type that prefers to work as a farmer or a builder. A more refined hand of a similar type is the Metal hand, which is also square in shape. A metal hand belongs to a determined and obstinate person who has a good head for business.

Links

The Chinese use a map of the hand in much the same way as Westerners do, but they link the positions on the hand to the trigrams of the I Ching. They also lump together two of the mounts that Westerners view separately. The following illustrations show the mounts with their western and their Chinese names.

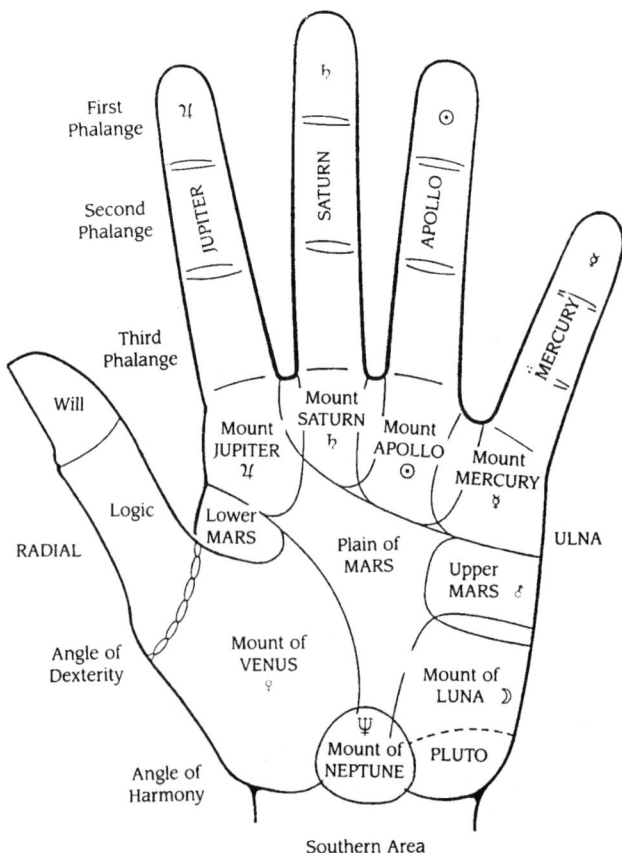

Southern Area

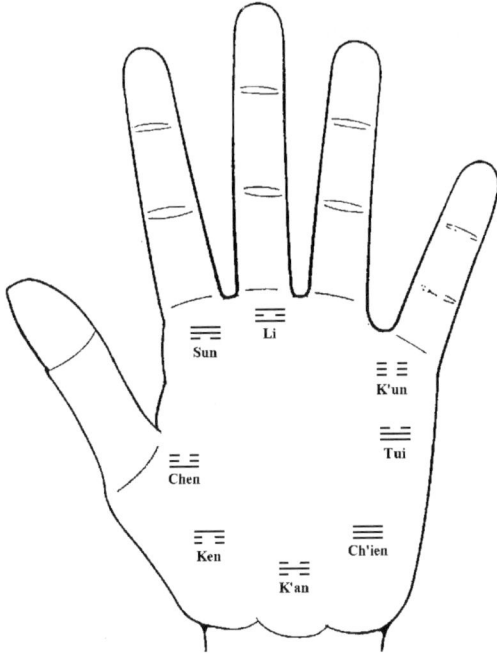

At this point, hand reading becomes inextricably linked to the I Ching and the familiar concepts that all Chinese diviners understand. The following table shows how the ideas are linked. The numbers in the far left-hand column refer to the position of each trigram on the hand.

In this book, I have only considered the Chinese view of the mounts. At this point, you can choose to buy books that take you further into Chinese hand reading, or to adapt the lines and marks of Western hand reading by using the Chinese mounts along with them. For example, a strong line on the mount of Saturn is an indication of wealth in later life, by either Eastern or Western methods of hand reading. In fact, there seems to be much agreement between the systems in general.

Number	Trigram	Name	Type of energy	Interpretation
One	Li	Fire	Summer, abundance	Fame
Two	K'un	Earth	Nourishment, nurturing	Mother and eldest daughter
Three	Tui	Lake	Joy, legacies	Wife, mistress, children
Four	Ch'ien	Heaven	Masculinity, authority	Father and eldest son
Five	K'an	Water	Winter, danger, hardship	Inheritance
Six	Ken	Mountain	Family, obstacles	Brothers
Seven	Chen	Thunder	Roads, rivers, travel	Education
Eight	Sun	Wind/Wood	Growth, expansion	Wealth
Nine	Ming T'ang	Emperor	Center, health	Health

Interpretations

One - Li

This area of the hand is concerned with wealth, abundance and the image of summer when the crops are beginning to be harvested. If this is prominent, it brings a comfortable life, but when flat, the person could be impoverished in old age. This area is said to rule the middle 25 years of life. The Mount of Li lumps together the western Mounts of Saturn and Apollo, which also talk about the accumulation of money and property, but we see this as having more to do with middle and old age than the Chinese do.

Two - K'un

This area is said to rule the last 25 years of life. K'un always represents the mother figure to the Chinese, both in the sense of a nurturer but also as a ruler of the extended family. It is the female part of the hand and it shows the condition of marriage on a man's hand, while on a woman's hand it refers to children and domestic life. There is a connection between east and west here, as Westerners look at marriage and children for both partners in this part of the hand. We call this the Mount of Mercury and we link this to relationships, but also to communications ability, literary talent, educational interests and computer literacy.

Three - Tui

This area rules leisure and retirement. If high, it suggests that the person will become rich through his work and that he or she will employ others. Legacies, marriage or a gamble paying off could lead to riches. If the area is flat, the person is likely to be either wasteful or unlucky. Westerners see this Mount of Mars relating to energy, courage and the ability to confront or stand up to others. This area also relates to the end of the head line, and thus to more or less the same ideas as in Chinese palmistry, especially career matters.

Four - Ch'ien

The Chinese regard Ch'ien as the father figure and the seat of authority in the family. This part of the hand is considered to be strongly masculine and it determines whether a man and his sons will do well in their careers, and whether they will obtain good jobs, gain promotion, status and be well paid or not. If prominent, the news is good, if flat and weak looking, the man won't get far in life and he may not be blessed with sons. Westerners see this as the mount of the Moon, which relates to creativity, imagination and travel.

Five - K'an

If this area of the hand is high it can signify inheritance, but if flat, it suggests a life of hardship. Western palmists call this the Mount of Neptune; we see this as having something to do with health and the ability to bear children, also the bridge between the material and spiritual world.

Six - Ken

The Chinese use this area to see if the person has brothers, sisters and friends. If high, he will have many such connections, but if flat, there will be few. Westerners call this area the Mount of Venus and apart from a link to sensuality, possessions and a love of music, the two systems tend to agree here.

Seven - Chen

The Chinese see this area in connection with fortune and fame. It relates to travel and to success. If high, it promises wealth, but if thin and pale, there will be sorrow and losses. There is some connection here, as this Venus area symbolizes energy to a western palmist, and if there is no energy, the subject is not likely to be successful. We also see this as a wealth indicator.

Eight - Sun

This area represents growth and expansion to the Chinese, and it can relate to wealth through steady, careful management and also respect within the community. If high, the chances of a steady climb to success are good, if flat and pale, this is less so. This area also refers to the first 25 years of life, and if it is higher than Li or K'un, the subject will have a good start in life but he may dissipate his funds later on. It suggests that a woman with a good mount here would help her husband in his business affairs. To Westerners, this Mount of Jupiter deals with ambition and success, self-belief, idealism and wisdom. Westerners note that a person with a heart line that runs across the hand in a straight line and ends in the middle of this mount will seek out a partner who has money, status, education, the "right" culture or religion etc., so the two systems agree here

Nine - Ming T'ang or Five Stars field

This is the centre of the palm, the area that Westerners call the Plain of Mars. To the Chinese, this area is concerned with health and daily luck. Western palmists look all over the hand for health problems, and this area of the hand is important because it contains a good many lines and marks, especially much of the all-important fate and Apollo lines that are used so much in the predictive side of palmistry. Some Chinese readers use the condition of the centre of the hand as an oracle by looking at such things as temporary discoloration or vague marks. This kind of clairvoyant or intuitive palmistry is not unknown in the west, but most western palmists prefer to read the lines than to look for temporary changes that appear on the hand. Oddly enough, I am one of those people who does look at temporary changes, especially red patches on a hand at the time of a reading; these often guide me to a specific line or area of the hand, thus giving me guidance as to what is troubling the client at that point in time.

SEVEN

The I Ching

Changing lines - preparing for your reading - divining with the coins - the Hexagrams - interpreting the I Ching - the trigrams - some of the complexities - individual lines - static & changing lines - the egg-head section

The words "I Ching" are pronounced Eee Ching or Yee Ching, or even Yee Ging. It is a fortune telling oracle that also gives advice from the gods and ancestors. The word "Ching" means scroll, although nowadays this is usually translated as book. The word "I" translates as concerning calamity and disaster. Despite this rather upsetting interpretation, the system is designed to help a person to cope with the trials and tribulations of normal life. The I Ching system provides information, wisdom, virtue, warning, advice and caution. While many I Ching readings seem to be about progress or hindrance in one's life path, they don't always specify whether this relates to work, relationships, domestic life, finances or any other specific matter. It is frequently left up to the questioner to apply the advice to their particular situation.

Changing lines

The I Ching is known in the west as the "Book of Changes". While it is true that one tends to consult any form of divination at times of change and uncertainty, this is not the reason for the strange name. As you will see towards the end of this chapter, the lines of the I Ching move or change, in a formalized and traditional manner.

Preparing for your Hexagram reading

Before you begin your reading, ensure that the table you intend to use is clear of clutter and mundane things, and cover it with a clean cloth. Keep your tools and your I Ching book in a special utensil, which you should store on a shelf that is higher than your head. Before your reading, light three joss sticks, hold them in both hands and bow three times to your personal God or to the Lord Buddha, and then pray for guidance. This will remove you from the activities of daily life and put you in a meditative frame of mind. This will also create a link with the gods and ancestors who will guide and advise you.

Divining with I Ching coins

If using coins, you will need three coins for your readings. If you decide to buy some imitation Chinese coins from a Chinese shop, consider the heavily decorated sides for tails (Yin). If you cannot find Chinese coins, buy some newly minted coins of a small denomination in your own local currency, and keep them in your I Ching equipment box. Treat the heads as Yang, and tails as Yin. Once you have made your preparations, hold the coins in both hands and shake them a little, then throw them down on the table.

After you have thrown the coins, see whether you have a majority of heads or tails. If the majority of coins are heads, this gives a Yang reading and you need to note down an unbroken line on a piece of paper. If the throw gives you a majority of tails, note down a broken Yin line. Your second throw will give you a second line, which should be drawn above the first. Your third line should be drawn above the second, and so on until you have six lines, which will make up your hexagram as shown in the following example.

```
━━━━━━━━━
━━━━━━━━━
━━━  ━━━
━━━━━━━━━
━━━━━━━━━
━━━━━━━━━
```
9

Now look through the diagrams in the following table show-ing all 64 hexagrams, and see which one you have drawn. Note down the number of the hexagram and look up its meaning in the pages that follow the table.

Using Yarrow sticks

If you want to be more "Chinese" and use sticks for your reading, you can do so. Wooden vases containing sticks (which, nowadays, are actually unlikely to be made from yarrow) are sold in Chinese areas and tourist shops. Each stick is numbered both in Chinese and in English. Prepare for your I Ching reading in the same way as I outlined above, then take the vase, hold it out hori-zontally in front of you and shake it until a few sticks protrude. Take the three sticks that protrude the furthest and consider the numbers written on them. Odd numbers represent Yang and even numbers represent Yin. From there, it is easy to continue as per the instruc-tions for throwing coins.

Later in this chapter, I will go into the trigrams and also tell you how to discover which lines should change, which should re-main static, and also what to do with these lines.

A table of the 64 hexagrams follows.

The Hexagrams of the I Ching

1 2 3 4

5 6 7 8

9 10 11 12

13 14 15 16

17 18 19 20

21 22 23 24

25 26 27 28

29 30 31 32

| 33 | 34 | 35 | 36 |

| 37 | 38 | 39 | 40 |

| 41 | 42 | 43 | 44 |

| 45 | 46 | 47 | 48 |

| 49 | 50 | 51 | 52 |

| 53 | 54 | 55 | 56 |

| 57 | 58 | 59 | 60 |

| 61 | 62 | 63 | 64 |

Interpreting the I Ching

I have modernized the interpretations a little, for them to be meaningful to western readers, but I have kept the rather lovely original names for each of the hexagrams.

1. Ch'ien

Creativity, the King

This hexagram is pure Yang, it is made up of two Ch'ien trigrams. It is the most masculine, fatherly and muscular of the hexagrams. This means that you will have to act with courage and confidence, focus on your goals and go all out for what you want. Initiate new ideas and use your energy wisely. In business you will need to show leadership and strength, while in your personal life your loved ones will turn to you for direction. Use your strength wisely and don't be aggressive or obstinate. This powerful hexagram could refer to the opening of an important new phase in your life.

2. K'un

Receptivity, the Queen

This hexagram doubles the trigram, K'un, and it is the most motherly and feminine of the hexagrams. Adjust to circumstances, fit in and don't make waves. To some extent, your future happiness is in the hands of others or it will involve others, so don't think only of yourself. This is a powerful hexagram, but it emphasizes the feminine virtues of endurance, duty, fitting in and waiting for things to come right. Go with the flow for a while and use your intuition.

3. Chun

Difficulty at the start

You are at the beginning of a new phase and you don't know where this will lead. You must break new ground now and while new projects will get off to a slow start, they will improve. Expect to reach your goals in a slow and steady manner. A new relationship might be in the air.

4. Meng

Youth, folly, inexperience

You need to gain or update skills or to obtain an education. Take advice and learn slowly. If you are misunderstood, take the time to explain yourself to others. Don't put on airs and graces, and be ready to listen to wise words. Treat others kindly and generously.

5. Hsu

Waiting

There is danger ahead, so don't plunge into anything. If life is quiet now, take a rest and wait for busier times to come. Meditate for inner wisdom and listen to the advice of sincere friends. Ambition and advancement are on the way, even if they are not evident just yet. It may be beneficial to cross water for business or personal reasons.

6. Sung

Conflict

Although you are probably in the right, this is not a good time to argue or to state your point. Accept criticism or a lack of credit for work done, just for the moment. Don't attempt large undertakings in business or elsewhere, because maintaining a steady course is the best option. Asking for advice is wise. Love and marriage are not favorable at the moment.

7. Shih

The army, collective force, leadership

A battle is ahead and you need to strive to maintain the confidence of those who depend upon you. Others are on hand to help you and spiritual guidance is also close by. You have to decide whether you should fight against injustice or retreat.

8. Pi

Union, joining

You need to join others in a collective campaign of some kind. You may need to pull together at work or in the family, and also to work for the good of those around you as well as for yourself. This is a favorable time for trust in business and also for love and marriage.

9. Hsiao Ch'u

Taming small powers, restraint

Times may be hard for a while, but with a sensible and economic approach you will achieve your aims and appreciate the good times all the more when they arrive. Restraint, sincerity and regard for others will be needed. If a relationship or some other situation is not working out, you may have to leave it.   *Oct 22*

10. Lu

Treading, caution

Leave things as they are until more favorable conditions apply. Be firm, even with yourself, and tread the straight and narrow path. Don't allow others to take advantage of you or to force you to lose your stride. Use intuition.

11. T'ai

Peace, harmony, prosperity

A time of peace, harmony and happiness. Share your happiness and good fortune with those who are less well off. This is a time to plant for the future or harvest from the past.

12. P'i

Stagnation, disharmony

Poverty, losses and hard times are around you now, but a change in outlook or attitude will help. Do not be discouraged, because sometimes out of misfortune good things emerge. Relationships are difficult now. Be modest and don't make a fuss.

13. T'ung Jen

Fellowship of men, community

Teamwork is the key to success, although you may need to become the leader of the team. Competitors and battles in business will occur, but there is light at the end of the tunnel. You will soon be able to make better progress and pass from obscurity to a brighter and more successful future. Success is yours but you must share the benefits of this with others, and do things with colleagues if you can.

14. Ta Yu

Great possessions, wealth

You will soon be doing very well, but you may incur jealousy or make small losses through not watching the pennies enough. Riches, wealth and success are assured. Work and study will go together and you will soon be in a better position to understand the tasks ahead of you. Don't go overboard in trying to impress others, just grasp the basics and get on with your job quietly.

15. Ch'ien

Modesty, moderation

Avoid extremes and try to achieve a balance in your life. Be modest but don't be stupidly humble, or allow others to make you a victim.

16. Yu

Happiness, enthusiasm

Despite the Chinese title of happiness, the reading for this hexagram is that of preparation and having the enthusiasm to set out on a new project. You must ensure that all is in order and that there are no loose ends left hanging before you make a start. You will need to advertise yourself and your wares, and to create an enthusiastic atmosphere. Don't fall for your own propaganda.

17. Sui

Following, adapting

This is a good time for marriage and personal life, but not a fortunate time for business affairs or friendship, although some new friends can be made at this time. In business it would be best to drift with the current, and to allow others to show you the way or take the initiative on your behalf. You will be in charge of your own affairs again soon enough.

18. Ku

Repairing, clearing out rot and decay, revising

Losses, setbacks and hardship are all around, and whether it is finances, business or a matter of the heart that is on your mind, trouble seems to be all around. A change of attitude will help matters greatly and a change of luck is on the way. You will have to put right something that is wrong and you may have to apologize for an error or an injustice or in order to correct a misunderstanding. Be scrupulously honest in all your dealings and be seen to be in the right.

19. Lin

Approach, promotion, gathering strength

Just as a King deals with his subjects magnanimously, so you must deal kindly with those who are under your control. You are, or soon will be, in an excellent position in life, so this is the time to be generous to others. Another interpretation tells us that a daughter should listen carefully to her mother and follow her advice. This hexagram also suggests that your luck will change for the better in the month of August.

20. Kuan

Observation, contemplation, understanding

Now is the time to take up a course of study or to train for something. It is also favorable to learn the art of meditation and to go on an inward journey or to analyze yourself. You will need to keep your eyes open for opportunities and in practical matters, and you will need to contemplate the wider issues. Don't take things on trust; look behind what is obvious and also use your intuition.

21. Shih Ho

Chewing, reform, biting through

Concentrate on the positive achievements that you have made, however small they may be, and refuse to allow others to stress the negative or unsuccessful aspects of your life. Don't allow petty jealousy from others to get you down. If a third person appears to be interfering in your marriage or in a personal relationship, keep cool as they will soon lose their influence and peace will return to your household.

22. Pi

Gracefulness, ornament

Dress nicely and look successful in order to sell an idea or to give an appearance of success. Once you have accomplished your aim, don't continue to live beyond your means, because there will soon be extra expenses and a slight shortage of money or opportunities. Contemplation and solitude will help to bring the equilibrium back into your life.

23. Po

Decay, disintegration

A man may have many girlfriends, but he could soon lose his money, looks, charisma - and eventually all the girlfriends as well. For women, this is a troublesome period when backstabbing and gossiping abounds. The odds are against you now. Some aspect of your life will be destroyed so that you can build afresh for the future. Guard against a situation where people who are close to you undermine you from the inside.

24. Fu

Return, turning point

Attune yourself to nature and to the seasons, and develop a sense of timing. A change of seasons will bring improvements and a renewal of energy. Be patient. Whether it is business matters, health or relationships, improvements are on the way. Reunions are likely. Oddly enough, this hexagram is not favorable for matters relating to first marriages, but it is good for subsequent ones.

25. Wu Wang

Innocence

Don't rush in where angels fear to tread. Be honest, stay within your own limitations and allow heaven to guide you. Be unselfish and uncomplicated and don't let temporary setbacks upset you. Take advice from your father, or follow the direction given by a respected leader, and good fortune will follow. An important undertaking is on the way.

26. Ta Ch'u

Taming the great powers

This hexagram represents power that is stored up and which, when released, can go far. You will soon make great advances in your career, and hard work and steady progress will bring success. Difficulties will be overcome; even difficult people can be used to your advantage.

27. I

Nourishment, provision

This is not a time for action. Take care of others and see that they are well fed and well looked after. Also take the opportunity to rest and build up physical strength for times of action. If every part of an enterprise works together in the right rhythm, much can be accomplished, otherwise losses result.

28. *Ta Kuo*

Great excess, weight, inner strength

A heavy branch breaks when it is overloaded, so you shouldn't take on too much at this time. It is better to know your limitations and to work within them. In business, this is a warning against too much expansion or working too hard. This hexagram also advises caution to those who are thinking of taking up with a younger lover or of rescuing one with problems. If you need an escape route, one will open up now.

29. *K'an*

Water, a ravine, danger

In most western systems, water is seen to be something pleasant that gently flows along, but Chinese rivers are huge and they can be moody and dangerous, so water is treated with caution. This hexagram suggests that there are pitfalls ahead and possibly even danger. Don't take risks and avoid decision-making. Guard against theft, trickery and misuse of alcohol. Women will have menstrual or other female problems soon. Keep the lines of communication open.

30. *Li*

Fire, clarity

In the west, fire is seen as dangerous, but the Chinese see it as a source of light and thus also of knowledge. Intellectual pursuits will go well and an intellectual approach to anything will be helpful. Passion is likely to rule your head, and whether this influences a business decision or a matter of the heart, common sense is advised. This is favorable if it takes place in the summer, unfavorable in the autumn.

31. *Hsien*

Attraction, relating

An attraction will bring people together and this could mean the start of a blissful love affair or a successful business partnership. Avoid pressing others into doing what you want unless they want it as well. Don't envy those who seem cleverer or more successful than you are; remember, the bigger they are, the harder they fall.

32. Heng

Duration, perseverance, enduring

Stay put, persevere and allow things to take their course. Hastiness will bring problems. Don't insist on having things all your own way.

33. Tun

Retreat

Sometimes one has to step backwards for a while. Business may be poor, and you must not throw good money after bad. It is a bad time to embark on a love relationship or indeed, anything new right now. There are crafty people around you who will seek to take advantage of you, so watch out for traps and don't fall into them. You may have to use some guile yourself in order to slide out of a tricky situation.

34. Ta Chuang

Great power

If you have to use strong words, back them up with meaningful action, or you will not be taken seriously. Take the initiative and make an effort to succeed, but don't be forceful when it isn't actually necessary. Treat lovers gently and avoid throwing your weight around in the home.

35. Chin

Progress, advancement

Your fortunes are improving and you are on the way up. Be honest in all your dealings, and also be open so that jealous people will not be able to point fingers. An excellent hexagram to find for those in business; in career matters, it suggests that promotion and success are on the way, but don't take an aggressive stance.

36. Ming I

Darkening of the light

When depression and hard times arrive, be cautious and restrained but don't allow yourself to become ground down by misery. Wait, because things will improve. Just do what needs to be done and refrain from moaning to others about your troubles. Retreat from life a little. Study and train yourself for something new. Keep secrets.

37. Chia Jen

The family

Family life and domestic circumstances take precedence for a while, and you will need to cooperate with other family members. Attend to your normal daily duties, make your surroundings comfortable and your situation happier. Deal with problems right away rather than trying to escape from them.

38. K'uei

Opposition, contradiction

Be flexible and allow some leeway to others. Even if you know you are right, don't ram the fact down the throats of others. Expect opposition from colleagues at work and from family members in the near future. Perhaps it would be best to keep quiet and try to fit in for a while.

39. Chien

Obstruction, difficulties

This is a bad time for practically anything and it is a particularly difficult time for love relationships. Don't moan, get help if you can and wait for better times.

40. Hsieh

Liberation

An acute situation will come to a head and you will know where you stand. Free yourself from unnecessary encumbrances so that you are in a position to move forward confidently. If you need a job you will find it, and if anything else is holding you back, it won't be for long.

41. Sun

Decrease

Something is about to cost you money; perhaps a tax bill is on the way. You might have to spend money on others or you may choose to help others out. If you don't give to others now, the laws of karma suggest that something will be taken from you.

42. I

Benefit, harvest, increase

In times like these, even a total incompetent can succeed. Business and finances are on the way up and love or marriage could come your way soon.

43. Kuai

Determination

The outlook for financial and career matters is good, but it would be worth taking out insurance policies of some kind. Don't allow bad behavior to destroy what you have achieved. Love affairs are likely to be difficult, with quarrels spoiling the atmosphere.

44. Kou

Encountering, temptation

This hexagram is mainly concerned with relationship matters. This is a good time to flirt a little, to try dating a number of different people and to enjoy the social side of life, although serious commitments don't seem to be in the air right now. Business matters prosper, but in both business and social life you should avoid being influenced by others. Calm persuasion will help you to influence others.

45. Ts'ui

Gathering, assembling

Personal relationships should be happy and there could be a family celebration in the air. Work is all right, too. Don't be awkward, just go along with the crowd and the general mood for the time being.

46. Sheng

Ascending, advancing

Don't give up; move steadily onwards, because progress can be made now. Your efforts will be rewarded and creative enterprises will be successful. You can bring bad luck upon yourself if you are arrogant, boastful or unpleasant to others. Much the same goes for love and marriage.

47. K'un

Oppression, adversity

There will be hard times soon, so look within yourself to find the strength to cope with them. Adversity can sometimes be character building. Have confidence, don't beat your head against the wall, stay calm and cope as well as you can.

48. Ching

The well

Work may be monotonous, but it has to be done. Share any benefits that you have accrued with others, but watch that they don't take the credit for your efforts or put difficulties in your way. If you have to choose between people or between paths, use your intuition and avoid those who are dishonest.

49. Ko

Revolution, change

The wheel of fortune is turning and you may move house or change your job soon. Divorce, marriage or even political changes are in the air. Your outer manner and presentation will improve, and you will soon be able to impress others.

50. Ting

The caldron

Ancient people looked after their cooking pots and other tools because they couldn't pop out to the shops and replace them easily. Ensure that your tools, equipment and vehicles are in working order. Don't worry about small mishaps but guard against larger ones. Take vitamins, eat well and cook something nice for those who you love.

51. Chen

Thunder, shock, turmoil

This is a repeat of the thunder trigram, and it signifies that there is stormy weather ahead. Don't panic, just wait until it passes and then reassess your situation. Oddly enough, this is a good hexagram for anyone who communicates for a living.

52. Ken

Stillness, keeping calm

This repeats the stillness trigram, so it suggests that you take things easily and progress slowly along your present path. Don't take unnecessary gambles or more difficult jobs than those you are already coping with. Peace, love and harmony can be expected at home.

52. Chien

Gradual development

Happiness will be assured in love or marriage, as long as you keep to the rules and don't embark on a fling. In all other things, develop slowly, even though there doesn't seem to be much progress at the moment.

54. Kuei Mei

The marrying girl, the maiden

Chinese marriages were (and often still are) arranged ones. Worse still, the girl had to go and live with the husband's family and put up with whatever they did to her. This could work out well, but often it was a recipe for victimization. Thus, this hexagram counsels against getting into a situation that you can't get out of quickly, especially marrying or becoming entangled in an affair. Also, try to avoid situations at work and elsewhere where you are likely to be made into a victim. New relationships are doomed to disaster, quarrels and heartbreak. If you cannot get what you want, then at least want what you already have. This refers to matters of love, sex and also to business or financial decisions.

55. Feng

Greatness, prosperity, abundance

You will be inwardly happy and troubles that come from outside will not be able to harm you. Success, brilliance and prosperity are indicated, but there is a strong warning not to overexpand or to overstep the mark. This is a good time to consolidate your gains, but not to lay out money on new ventures.

56. Lu

The exile, travel   ✓ Nov 2024

In the ancient world, travelling was arduous and dangerous and it meant being out of touch with colleagues and loved ones. Today we girdle the globe without a second thought. This is a good time to travel on business or pleasure, or perhaps even to run away from home! In short, get out and about and see what the world has to offer. You will need to market yourself soon, possibly while looking for a new job. Improve your manner and your appearance and be careful with whom you associate.

57. Sun

Penetration, persistence, gentleness

Yet another duplicate of a trigram. This one suggests that you must persevere with what you are doing, be reasonable and others will accept your ideas. This is an excellent time for those who travel on business or those who need to deal with people in other lands. All travel is well starred at the moment. Bend with the wind and don't be argumentative.

58. Tui

Joy

This is a great time for all manner of career and financial matters, especially those that involve communicating with others. Careers that rely upon talking, singing, acting, teaching or diplomacy will succeed now. Inner contentment will be reflected outwardly to others and outer harmony will generate inner peace.

59. Huan

Dispersion, reunification

This may mean a move of house, a new venture in business, a change of job, a new car or recovery from illness. This is a great time to alter your attitudes and to brush up your appearance. A family may become scattered, but this is due to one or two of its members stretching their wings or moving on in order to improve their prospects. Marriage and relationships will be put on the back burner for a while, because you will be too busy travelling and working to concentrate on these matters.

60. Chieh

Limitation

You need to be cautious and to accept certain limitations. Reserves of energy, goods or money will be needed while you sit out a difficult situation. When doors open, you will be able to move forward through them, but for now, go by the rules - even if they are someone else's.

61. Chung Fu

Inner truthfulness

Be true to yourself and sincere towards others, in order to gain their trust. This hexagram predicts a time of great changes for the better in your career, business and financial matters, and especially matters of the heart. A move of house or across water is possible, and a change of scene will be beneficial. There may be stormy weather ahead, but this is probably due to all the turmoil that upheavals of this magnitude are sure to bring.

62. Ksiao Kuo

Slight excess, moderation

Your progress will be halted, and this may be due to external forces or your own feelings of negativity or fear. Don't be a miser, give generously of your time and your resources and these will be repaid. Don't waste your energy or get into a panic needlessly. If storms arrive, stay safe and wait for them to pass.

63. Chi Chi

Completion

A cycle has ended. You should work to consolidate what you have achieved thus far in order to build for the future. You must guard against stupidly losing all that you have gained. Marriage or a serious relationship are favorable at this time, possibly because the courtship phase has been completed.

64. Wei Chi

Before completion

The previous hexagram is called Completion, and now we have one that is called Before Completion! This situation is very similar to the two last Tarot cards in the Major Arcana pack, which are Judgement and The World. Spiritually speaking, this is like the end of life, but the start of a new phase in heaven or even a new incarnation. In practical terms, you must finish the project in hand.

Perhaps you have a final exam to revise for, or things to throw out prior to a move. Something new will soon come along.

THE TRIGRAMS OF THE I CHING

The eight trigrams of the I Ching describe the various aspects of the natural world as seen by the ancients. They describe aspects of the family, parts of the body, human behavior, directions, times of the year, colors, animal associations and much more. This is similar to the way western astrologers use the signs and planets. The trigrams cover every combination from fully Yang to fully Yin.

The method

The method for finding your trigram is the same as described earlier, in the section on hexagrams. You will need three coins, a pen and some paper.

Form a question in your mind and hold the coins in your hands for a moment, then throw them down and see whether you have a majority of heads or tails.

If heads are in the majority, your first line will be an unbroken Yang line.

If tails are in the majority you must draw a broken Yin line.

This will be the lowest line of your trigram. Repeat the process twice more to find the middle line and the top line. The resulting trigram should give a clue as to the solution of your problem.

Connections

Throughout this book we see connections between many of the divinations, with the elements being important to such things as astrology and Feng Shui. If you work your way through other chapters of this book, especially those on Astrology, the Four Pillars, Feng Shui and the Lo Shu, you will find these ideas coming into play time and again.

Ch'ien

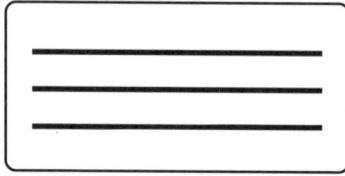

Trigram name	Heaven
Family member	Father
Body parts	Head, mind, cranium
Season	Late autumn
Direction	Northwest
Nature	Strong, creative
Color	White, gold
Plants	Chrysanthemums, herbs
Trees	Fruit trees
Animals	Horse, lion, tiger

Chi'en is one of the two most powerful trigrams. It is pure Yang, extremely masculine and it represents action, drive and energy. Ch'ien represents the power of heaven or the power that is held by the head of a family or the head of an organization. This trigram represents power, strength, creativity, logic and courage. It suggests a time when you focus your mind and your energies on a particular goal in order to achieve your particular ambition. This can refer to a career matter, working for an exam, writing a book, actively searching for love, becoming a swimming champion, walking a marathon, getting pregnant or achieving any kind of ambition you may have in mind.

To a western astrologer, Chi'en is like a combination of Mars and Saturn, combining the masculine action of Mars, the authority of Saturn and also the Saturnian ability to focus on a goal.

K'un

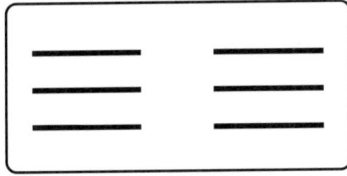

Trigram name	Earth
Family member	Mother
Body parts	Stomach, abdomen, womb
Season	Late summer
Direction	Southwest
Nature	Patient, devoted
Color	Black, dark colors
Plants	Potatoes, roots and bulbs
Trees	Trunks of trees
Animals	Ox, mare, cow, ant

K'un is the most feminine of the trigrams and it represents the feminine attributes of care, nurture and consideration for others. K'un relates to feelings and intuition, and the key ideas are of receptivity, endurance and acceptance, docility and patience. One typically Chinese image is that of potatoes and root vegetables, because they mature in late summer and they can be stored for the winter, as opposed to something fragile that must be used up immediately. This trigram relates to mother figures of all kinds but it also relates to ordinary people - as opposed to important or special people.

To western astrologers, K'un links perfectly with the moon.

Chen

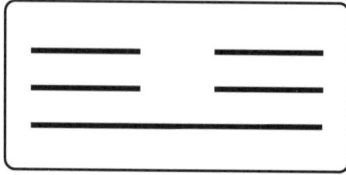

Trigram name	Thunder
Family member	Eldest son
Body parts	Foot, voice
Season	Spring
Direction	East
Nature	Strong, mobile
Color	Yellow
Plants	Flowers, blossoms
Trees	Evergreens, blossoms, bamboo
Animals	Dragon, eagle, swallow

Chen is associated with regeneration. After a period of drought, a thunderstorm brings welcome rain, but lightning can also be destructive. This represents male arousal and sexuality, fertility, initiative, action and energy. It represents men who are young or middle aged but not elderly. The image here is a strong worker, leader, possibly an artist, or an inventor.

To a western astrologer, Chen represents Mars.

Kan

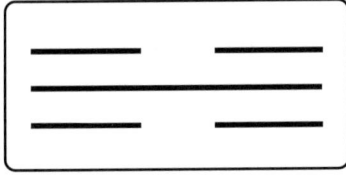

Trigram name	Water
Family member	Middle son
Body parts	Ear, kidneys
Season	Winter
Direction	North
Nature	Dangerous, cunning
Color	Blue
Plants	Reeds, water plants
Trees	Willow, alder
Animals	Pig, rat

K'an represents turning points or times when one is not in control of events. Uncertainty, unpredictable times, danger and stress are indicated here. If other symbols are favorable, such change is accepted as a challenge; if not, then it is feared. Hard times are all around and desire is unlikely to be fulfilled for the time being. It represents young men, especially aggressive or difficult ones, and also fishermen.

To a western astrologer, K'an is similar to Uranus and possibly Pluto, but the reference to fishermen also represents the power of the sea and the destructive side of Neptune.

Ken

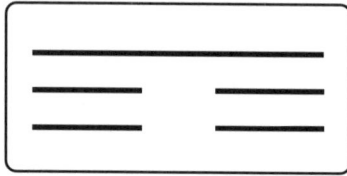

Trigram name | Mountain
Family member | Youngest son
Body parts | Hand, spine
Season | Early spring
Direction | Northeast
Nature | Still, quiet
Colors | Violet
Plants | Alpine plants
Trees | Nuts, olives, old trees
Animals | Dog, bull, leopard, mouse

Ken represents a time of retreat and reflection when spiritual issues take precedence over worldly ones. A person may forget earthly concerns and concentrate on religious or philosophical ideas, travelling on a strictly spiritual pathway for a while. This is a time of silence, aloneness, withdrawal from life and stillness. The people represented here are those who seek seclusion or who find themselves secluded, thus priests, monks, prisoners and probably sick people as well. This also represents male children up to the age of 16.

To a western astrologer, Ken is very much like Neptune.

Sun

```
━━━━━━━━━━━━━
━━━━━━━━━━━━━
━━━━━    ━━━━━
```

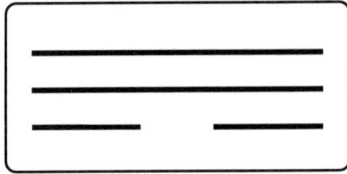

Trigram name	Wind (also Wood)
Family member	Eldest daughter
Body parts	Thigh, upper arm, lungs, nerves
Season	Early summer
Direction	Southeast
Nature	Gentle, adaptable
Color	Green
Plants	Grass, poppies, lilies
Trees	Tall trees
Animals	Rooster, snake, tiger

Sun represents slow growth and gradual change for the better. It represents feminine virtues of endurance, gentle determination, adaptability and fair play. Sun represents women up to middle age, those who travel, teachers and business people.

The nearest association for a western astrologer to grasp here is a combination of Mercury and Venus.

Li

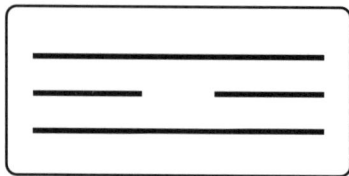

Trigram name	Fire
Family member	Middle daughter
Body parts	Eyes, blood, heart
Season	Summer
Direction	South
Nature	Beautiful, intelligent
Color	Orange
Plants	Tomatoes, peppers
Trees	Dried out trees
Animals	Pheasant, turtle, goldfish

The settlements of Northern China that eventually became Beijing, Tiensing and Nanking were always cold in the winter. Ancient rural communities welcomed the hot weather and the harvest that followed.

Li represents illumination and inspiration, clarity and knowledge. It is associated with young women, craftsmen, artists and those who are generous and big hearted.

To a western astrologer, this is like the sun and Mercury.

Tui

```
━━━━━    ━━  ━━
━━━━━━━━━━━━━
━━━━━━━━━━━━━
```

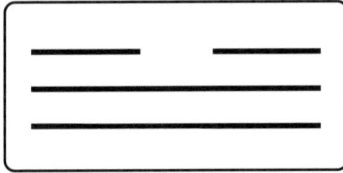

Trigram name	Lake
Family member	Youngest daughter
Body parts	Mouth, lips
Season	Autumn
Direction	West
Nature	Joyful, sensual
Color	Red
Plants	Magnolia, gardenia
Trees	Mangrove, seaside trees
Animals	Sheep, birds, antelope

Think of autumn and ripe sensuality. A good harvest is always welcome.

Tui represents the inner psychic world and it is associated with healing, magic, joy and pleasure. As a person, it links with girls under the age of 16, daughters and oddly enough, mistresses - thus women with no real power in the family as such.

There is no clear link with western astrology here, although some attributes of Neptune and even Mercury might apply.

An explanation of some of the complexities

The I Ching is known as the Book of Changes. One kind of change occurs when any of the trigrams is paired with any other trigram. There are eight trigrams and the total number of permutations when pairing each trigram is 64 (8 x 8 = 64), which is why there are 64 hexagram readings.

Each trigram has a meaning, but when two are put together, a combined meaning emerges. If, for example, we were to team the pleasant trigram Sun or eldest daughter with the extremely unpleasant K'an or middle son, the effect is to create a hexagram that is called The Well. This signifies that one's well has become muddy and useless, suggesting that a situation has become extremely difficult. The only possible course of action is to do the right thing, to use one's intuition to avoid people who want to take advantage of one's good nature, but also to help the truly needy where possible. If one also takes into account the directions and times of the year indicated by the trigrams, and even the colors that are indicated, perhaps the gods could be encouraged to change one's circumstances for the better.

Much the same idea occurs in western astrology when two planets are in conjunction, because their two different energies become fused.

Individual lines

The original I Ching method is systematic and complicated. Every throw of the coins, each line, each number in a sequence of throws needs to be recorded before an answer can be given. In each hexagram, every line has a meaning that expands the basic reading.

In some systems, only those lines that refer to the class and status of the inquirer and the period of the inquirer's life are taken into account, and others are set aside. To give a modern day example, starting from the bottom upwards, the lowest line would refer to a young person who is training for a job or who is engaged in manual labor. A fairly youthful clerk or petty official might be assigned the second line up from the bottom, while a middle manager would be given the third. A mature board member would rise to line number four, while the Chairman or President of a company would be assigned number five. The wealthy and aged retiree who has put in his years at work and who is now looking forward to sailing and golfing during his remaining years, would be at the top of the hexagram heap. Age, status, wisdom and experience have always been revered in China. The reading could be left alone at this point, or the line selected could be used to form the bottom line of a new hexagram.

Static and changing lines

As I said in the introduction to this chapter, the I Ching is known as "The Book of Changes". This is not because we read the I Ching when our lives are in a state of flux, but because the system contains static and changing lines in addition to the main hexagrams. Unfortunately, there isn't room in this book to include these lines, so if you want to take this aspect further, you will have to treat yourself to a book that is specially devoted to the I Ching.

However, I can tell you how these lines are selected and how they change; believe me, that is hard enough to discover and to understand. So, if you do go on and study the I Ching further, at least you will know what you are supposed to be doing, and why.

If you buy a book on the I Ching, you will find that there is always some extra text that follows each hexagram reading. This text takes each of the six lines of the hexagram and gives a separate reading for each one If you try to read all six lines, you will discover that they give disjointed and possibly contradictory readings; this is because not all six lines should be read. To discover which lines are to be read, you need to take one further step right at the outset, when you throw your coins or pick your sticks.

As you already know, each line becomes Yang when a majority of heads are thrown, or Yin when a majority of tails are thrown. When all three coins are heads, or all three are tails (as opposed to two heads and a tail or vice versa), it is worth marking the end of the line with a small cross. The chances are that one or two of your six lines will emerge as "special" in this way, and these become your changing lines.

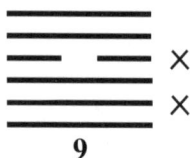

9

The following details show you the steps you need to take, from start to finish, and will make things clear and logical for you.

1. Treat yourself to an I Ching book or two, so that you have the full system on hand to consult.

2. Throw your coins, or pick up your sticks, and note down your Yang or Yin lines.

3. Those lines that are Yang or Yin due to all three coins having fallen with the same side up (or all three sticks with an odd or even number respectively) need to be marked with a small cross.

4. Read your hexagram as a whole.

5. Using your I Ching book, find the subsidiary lines that come after your main hexagram.

6. Remember that the hexagram is formed upwards, so line number one is the bottom line, number two is the one above, and so on.

7. Pick out the marked changing lines, and read the information given on those lines alone. For example, if line number four is your changing line, read that one and leave the rest.

8. *Now, swap lines that are Yang for Yin, and vice versa.* This forms a new hexagram.

9. Read your new hexagram.

10. Pick out the information for the lines that changed, and read that. Once again, if the only line that changed was number four, read that and leave the rest.

And finally, the egghead section - or how to build a computer,
Chinese style

The counting system that we use today is based on the original Roman system, with the Arabic addition of the zero. Our "base ten" system probably arose due to man's natural habit of counting on his thumbs and fingers, but it is not the only system that has been used. For example, Hebrew numerology uses letters of the alphabet, but not in tens, while the computer language that was developed by the American military in the 1960s used the binary system, which was set into groups of two. This ultramodern system is the one that powers every computer in use today, and takes space vehicles to the outer edges of our solar system. It may well have been inspired by the Pa Kua and the I Ching.

In a binary system, the numbers are organized in multiples of 2 instead of ten as in our normal decimal system; thus the sequence of multiples is expressed as 1,2,4,8,16,32,64,128, etc. while in our decimal system, the sequence would be 1, 10, 100, 1,000, etc.

An electrical contact switch can only be on or off, so the "switches" in a microchip can either be 0, which stands for off, or 1, which stands for on. This means that a binary number can be expressed as 10110101 or any similar combination of ones and zeros. By breaking the binary code, the number that I have just given would translate like this:-

1 = 128
0 = 0
1 = 32
1 = 16
0 = 0
1 = 4
0 = 0
1 = 1

Thus the sum would be 128+32+16+4+1 (=181).

Many thousands of such "bits" make up bytes, kilobytes, megabytes, gigabytes and any other amount of supersonic bits and bytes that a mind can conceive of. If you substitute the broken Yin line for the zero and the unbroken Yang line for the one, you have the binary code all ready and waiting to use.

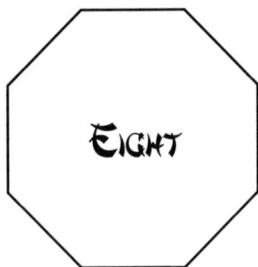

Eight

The Lunar Oracle

Background - procedure - interpretation - the Lunar Cycle - possible Tarot links

The lunar oracle resembles the kind of daily horoscope reading that we see in the stars columns of newspapers, but it is really only supposed to be consulted when something big is going on in one's life. The idea is that each day of the month is ruled by the position of the moon, and that by consulting the oracle you can see what a particular day will bring. It is especially useful if you want to make a start on something new, as it shows which days are auspicious for various kinds of activity.

Background

The system is rather fixed and categorical, which means that its value in a complex modern environment such as ours is limited. In ancient times, there may well have been useful and orderly benefits derived from this analysis of the moon cycle, and indeed, we still use the moon phases to guide us in many different areas, such as gardening, fishing and even when best to have medical treatment. The lunar oracle is therefore presented for you to experiment with, and to discover for yourself whether or not it works for you.

The procedure

The oracle runs from the first day of a new moon, through the 28-day cycle, to the last day of the old moon. Any decent diary, all desk diaries and many calendars show the phases of the moon, so it is simply a matter of finding the day of the new moon and counting onwards. If you like looking at the sky, you can spot the start of the new moon when the first sliver starts to show. If you are not sure which way round the new moon is, think of the word "DOC", because the new moon curves in the direction of the capital "D" and the old moon curves in the direction of the capital "C". As conditions are often too cloudy for sky watching, a decent diary is a must.

New   Crescent   Quarter   Gibbous

Full   Disseminating   Quarter   Balsamic

Interpretation

The oracle is very old and very Chinese, so some parts of it talk about an audience with the Emperor, the best time to flood a paddy field or the chances of an official being promoted by three ranks. I have modernized these ideas to make sense to a modern reader, but I have retained the Chinese titles of each reading in order to retain the flavor. Each day of the oracle refers to marriages and funerals and I have included these in the text because these events still occur fairly frequently in our own lives, although not as often as they did when families were larger. If two people decide to live together, they can take the starting date for this new partnership as a "marriage" as far as the oracle is concerned.

I have altered the original references to the birth of a baby under the general heading of starting something new. Such a new beginning may well refer to the birth of a child, but it could just as easily be the start of a new job, planting a crop, moving into a new house, opening a business or the start of a romance. Many of the readings refer to farm work and such things as planting or growing crops, or flooding paddy fields, and this reflects the rural nature of China. If you happen to be in farming, then this type of reading will fit your circumstances. In other cases, what you need to do is to use a little imagination in order to apply the readings to your own lifestyle, so that planting refers to the start of a particular cycle of work and so on.

Funerals and attending to the upkeep of a dead relative's tomb are important events in the Chinese calendar, as even nowadays the Chinese attach much importance to such things. They believe that the spirits of their ancestors can help them, so they continue to pay these ancestors respect and to look after their gravestones and tombs long after their death. This is close to the western Spiritualist idea of being able to obtain help from one's spiritual guides or even from one's dead relatives.

The Lunar Cycle, starting with the day of the new moon

Day one. The Horn
Anything that is started on this day will be successful and it will prosper. Intelligent people will move among influential people. Marriages will bring many children, but funerals or repairing tombs will be a sad affair.

Day two. The Neck
Don't start anything new today, because it will collapse within ten days. Don't allow your eldest child to take charge of anything important. Funerals and marriages will end in early deaths, and there is a risk of widows being left to cope alone.

Day three. The Root
A truly dreadful day in which marriages will come to naught, journeys over water will be a disaster and funerals will cause impoverishment.

Day four. The Chamber
Anything that is started today will bring wealth and prosperity, and the Spirits will protect it. Happiness, glory, longevity, honor and riches will ensue. Officials and people in positions of authority who attend funerals can expect a major promotion at their work or a rise in their status in society.

Day five. The Heart
This is a truly rotten day in which anything started will come to a bad end. Marriages and funerals are likely to be awful and they will result in three years of bad luck.

Day six. The Tail
This is a great day in which to make a start on an important enterprise, and this could bring a move to a head office, to the center of events or to a capital city. Anything to do with the growing of

crops will succeed and lead to long-term benefits. Funerals and marriages will enhance the standing of the family, and these could lead to better jobs or a better lifestyle in some unexpected way.

Day seven. The Basket

This is the time to build on anything that you have already started and also to put you shoulder to the wheel. An enterprise will bring good luck to your family. A great day for marriage, as the future is sure to bring prosperity to the couple. An auspicious day for repairing the tombs of your ancestors.

Day eight. The Ladle

Build upon what you have already started, as this will bring abundance and prosperity. Put a tomb in order, or celebrate a funeral to bring help and blessings from your ancestors. If you open a business or get moving on some farm work, this will be successful. A great day for starting a happy marriage.

Day nine. The Buffalo

Creative projects will come to nothing if they are started today. Neither marriage, business, farming nor anything else will succeed if it is begun now.

Day ten. The Woman

Relationship matters are badly starred today, especially those in the wider family. Brothers will fall out and women will either cause trouble or be hurt. A terrible time to marry or to bury someone.

Day eleven. The Void

The moral atmosphere in and around you is terrible and someone may embark upon a stupid affair. The women of the family need attention now, or they will start to look around for someone new. Children will be neglected.

Day twelve. The Roof

Don't take on any large enterprise today and be especially careful not to have an accident. Opening a business or irrigating a paddy field (or anything else for that matter), will only result in legal problems later on.

Day thirteen. The House

This is an excellent day in which to buy, alter or improve a house or to improve your land and livestock. Anything related to the family or to a family business will bring wealth and prosperity into the home. Marriages will succeed and funerals will bring luck from the ancestor in question.

Day fourteen. The Wall

This is a great day in which to make a start on anything. If you don't have a paddy field to irrigate, get the garden hose out and water the tomatoes!

Day fifteen. The Legs

Building work will be a great success today, but farming and business won't be. Happiness and harmony blow through the door of your home. A mysterious death could occur around this time.

Day sixteen. The Tie

A great day for marriage or childbirth, as descendants will do well in all spheres of life. Build something large now, as this will prosper.

Day seventeen. The Stomach

The Chinese people love the idea of having a full belly, because throughout their history there have been so many times when famine or shortages have made life intolerable. If you work on an enterprise today, it will ensure that you and your family have plenty to eat in the future. Riches and glory will result from your work today, while marriages will bring happiness and harmony.

Day eighteen. The Lights

A truly awful day in which to start anything. Leave everything for another day.

Day nineteen. The Thread

Whatever you start today will bring luck and blessings flowing through your door. Marriages and funerals will lead to a long life and happiness. Farming will bring success.

Day twenty. The Turtle

Don't get involved in anything awkward today, as this is likely to bring lawsuits and losses. If you refuse to heed this advice, three deaths will follow. Property matters are especially badly starred, and what you build may well fall down again.

Day twenty-one. The Three Associates

A great day for business and those who write, communicate or liaise with others will be extremely successful. Farming will succeed as well, but funerals or marriages will bring great unhappiness.

Day twenty-two. The Well

Any enterprise will bring money and numerous offspring to inherit the proceeds. Building work and animal husbandry will be successful. The family name will be respected now. If a person who has died a violent death is buried today, there will be trouble of some kind surrounding the event.

Day twenty-three. The Spirit

Don't deal in property, don't work on a property and don't get married today. Funerals will bring an increase in status, but not much else will succeed now.

Day twenty-four. The Willow

Guard against thieves and lawsuits. Don't build anything today. Funerals and marriages will be a miserable affair and the aftermath won't be any good either.

Day twenty-five. The Star

A great day in which to build or to work on your property or premises. The Chinese say that advancement will lead to the feet of the Emperor, which translated into modern terminology means that you are likely to become noticed by an important leader. If a man goes alone to attend a funeral or if he leaves the house to attend to the farm, his wife will take advantage of his absence and stray.

Day twenty-six. The Fishing Net

Any enterprise begun today will succeed and your descendants will build upon this success. Marriage will bring harmony and happiness. Funerals are likely to bring inheritance and help after the event, from the spirit of the dead person.

Day twenty-seven. The Wings

Construction of a tall building should be avoided, for this will bring the death of successive masters of the house. Marriages and funerals will lead to poverty. Young girls will run off with inappropriate boys.

Day twenty-eight. The Chariot

Any enterprise or job that you work on today will bring promotion and prosperity. Marriages will bring approval and blessings. Celebrating a funeral today will bring blessings from the spirit of the dead person.

A possible connection between this oracle and the Tarot

A very experienced Tarot reader once told me that an expert had suggested to her that Tarot cards originated in China. Well, nobody knows for sure where the ideas in the Tarot have from, and many would opt for ancient Egypt as their source. My feeling is that the Tarot themes are an amalgam of a number of ideas that have traveled from one spiritual center to another over the centuries, being absorbed and rearranged as they have gone along. However, whilst writing this book and immersing myself in Chinese mysteries, I am now more convinced than ever that some early form of the Tarot came from ancient China. This lunar oracle seems to show particularly strong links to the Tarot.

NINE

Mah Jong Reading

*Mah Jong sets - the suits - preparing for your read-
ing - interpreting the tiles - the Honors - Guardians*

Mah Jong is a very popular game in China and in any place
that Chinese people live. The Chinese gather in noisy Mah Jong
cafes and slap the Mah Jong tiles down onto the tables with happy
abandon. I have not played the game itself, and I understand that
can become complicated, but using Mah Jong for divination is not
at all difficult. The level at which you wish to understand the thinking behind the system is a matter of personal choice; you can either
take the reading at face value, or you can refer to some of the other
chapters in this book, such as those on the elements, the Lo Shu, I
Ching and astrology. As usual in this book, I have updated the readings so that they are of use in the modern world, but I have kept the
original Chinese references to animals, plants, etc.

Mah Jong sets

Modern Mah Jong sets are available in most cities where
there are any Chinese shops. They are usually made of rectangular
white plastic tiles about an inch and a half long, with intriguing
colored designs and marks printed on most of them, plus a few blank
tiles. There are also Mah Jong cards, but these are not as popular.
Older sets would have been made from ivory, bamboo or bone. The
designs on them are a cross between dominoes, Runes and playing

cards. Like so many Chinese divinations, they include directions, seasons and the symbols of the elements.

Here are examples of typical Mah Jong tiles:

The suits

The tiles are arranged in three suits, plus a few special tiles called the Honors and the Guardians.

This divination is amazingly similar to the Tarot. Two of the suits are close to those of the Tarot, especially the suit of Bamboo which is similar to the Tarot suit of Wands, and the suit of Circles which is strangely like the Tarot suit of Coins (also known as Pentacles). The way tiles can be added to a reading is also reminiscent of a Tarot reading. The major difference is that the Mah Jong contains four sets of everything (except for the Flowers and Seasons tiles), which is like dealing with four Tarot decks at once. If a particular tile is duplicated, this is an obvious indication that a particular issue or problem is emphasized or that it will persist, and this is especially so if it appears in more than one area of the spread.

If you are desperate to try the system and have no access to a Chinese shop, I suggest that you make some tiles by cutting card into small pieces and then write or draw designs to represent each of the Mah Jong symbols. If you are clever, patient and creative, you could use small stones or wood for your tiles.

This is how the Mah Jong set is made up:
Suit of Circles
Four sets of tiles, each numbered from 1 - 9
Suit of Bamboo
Four sets of tiles, each numbered from 1 - 9

Suit of Characters
Four sets of tiles, each numbered from 1 - 9
The Winds
Four sets of tiles, named North, East, South and West
The Dragons
Four sets of tiles, colored white, green and red

The Flowers
One set of tiles, named Plum, Orchid, Chrysanthemum and Bamboo
The Seasons
One set of four tiles, named Spring, Summer, Autumn and Winter

Preparing for your reading

Take all the tiles out of the box, place them face downwards and stir them around. Create a space in the middle of them, then select 13 tiles at random, keeping them face down. Give your 13 tiles an extra stir, and then divide them into four groups of three tiles, with one tile left over. Concentrate on your problem and the questions that you wish to have answered.

First:

1. Push three tiles away from you. These are the west tiles.
2. Pull three tiles towards you. These are the east tiles.
3. Push three tiles to your left. These are the north tiles.
4. Push three tiles to your right. These are the south tiles.
5. Place the remaining tile in the center, with the others arranged around it.

West

North   *South*

East

Next:

1. Turn the center tile over. If it is part of the Honors group, this has such special significance that it might answer your question straight away. This is very much like drawing a Major Arcana card in the Tarot.
2. The east row comes next; this refers to your personality and behavior, and it suggests areas of improvement or aspects of your current situation that need to be addressed.
3. The south row concerns the immediate outcome of your situation and can reveal the way that things will shortly be moving.
4. When looking at the west row, look at the two outer tiles, because these will tell you where your obstacles and difficulties lie.

The middle tile advises you on how to find your way out of your difficulties, and/or who might help you to do so.

5. The north row looks ahead 12 months, to show whether your present dilemma will be resolved and forgotten, if it will continue, or whether a completely new problem will soon beset you.

6. If a Guardian tile is turned up, you must take another tile at random from those outside the area of the spread and place it next to the Guardian tile. Guardian tiles suggest seasons, so this can help you to discover the timing of the events recorded in your reading. This also suggests that the Guardian tile protects the particular destiny shown by the new tile.

7. Watch for duplicated tiles; remember that they signify a particularly important facet of life and a problem that is unlikely to be resolved quickly.

INTERPRETING THE TILES

The Suit of Bamboo

Ace of Bamboo - Peacock
Success.

This tile can also signify a mature woman in a reading. If in the south, this suggests that an ambition will be achieved. If in the north, overconfidence.

Two of Bamboo - Duck
Faithfulness, a partnership.

A successful business or romantic relationship is on the way and this will bring enduring happiness. If surrounding tiles indicate problems, they will definitely refer to partnerships and relationships.

Three of Bamboo - Toad
Healing.

A good indicator of health, strength and recovery from sickness. If health is not an issue and if difficult tiles surround the Bamboo Toad, this indicates that the questioner is overreaching himself or asking for the unobtainable.

Four of Bamboo - Carp
Long life, peace.

This indicates peace after a time of trouble, and that recovery from illness, happiness and longevity are on the way.

Five of Bamboo - Lotus
Rebirth.

The start of a new phase. This might indicate the start of an enterprise or the actual birth of a child in the questioner's circle. Sorrow is passing away and goals can now be aimed for.

Six of Bamboo - Water
Travel, communications.

In all Chinese divinations, it is the flowing and moving element of Water that signifies communication. If this tile is drawn, travel and communications for business, personal life or pleasure are indicated. If near difficult tiles, expect delays and problems regarding travel.

Seven of Bamboo - Tortoise
Thought, knowledge and patience.

Progress is evident, although it seems to be slow going. Wisdom, knowledge and patience are very much associated with the Tortoise in Chinese mythology, so when this tile emerges, these things will need to be sought out or applied.

Eight of Bamboo - Mushroom
Eccentricity.

The questioner might have unusual talents, original ideas or a bizarre way of life. Life will be unpredictable and an unexpected event will occur.

Nine of Bamboo - Willow
Compliance.

In bad weather, the willow bends without breaking and it recovers later. It may be that old problems that have been left to fester need to be attended to immediately. In other cases, it is best to wait for a story to play itself out and to reach its own conclusion.

The Suit of Circles

Ace of Circles - Pearl
Wealth.
If surrounded by good tiles, finances are set to improve; otherwise this will need to be watched.

Two of Circles - Pine
A youth.
One meaning might be of creative or artistic success, but this tile can also refer to a young man who is a youthful relative. If the reading is being given for a woman, this may denote a lover. Depending upon surrounding tiles, this suggests a good outlook for love or a troublesome and dangerous love affair. A rival may soon arrive on the scene.

Three of Circles - Phoenix
Joy, virtue.
This signifies that everything will soon be straightforward, legitimate, correct and fair. Matters will proceed in the right way. There will soon be happiness and rejoicing.

Four of Circles - Jade
Perseverance.
The questioner will finish whatever he starts and he will then be able to congratulate himself on doing a job to everybody's satisfaction.

Five of Circles - Dragon
Good luck.
The lucky Dragon signifies good fortune in every type of divination, and the Mah Jong is no exception. However, it can offer a warning against losses through gambling and speculation.

Six of Circles - Peach
Feminine beauty.

This denotes a young woman who may be the sister of the questioner, a rival in love or even the questioner herself (depending upon her age). If allied to poor tiles, it suggests vanity, extravagance and too much money being spent on clothes and appearance. If with good tiles, it suggests success in an artistic endeavor.

Seven of Circles - Insect
Industriousness.

This shows that there is no escape from work; the chores and dull jobs have to be done, because if these are neglected, life becomes impossible. This suggests that the questioner isn't afraid of hard work, but it can warn against overwork, anxiety and tension.

Eight of Circles - Tiger
Man in uniform.

This may refer to an older man or one who is in a position of authority. This may denote a father, brother, boss or some other type of authority figure. Whether the person helps the questioner or is a source of conflict depends upon the surrounding tiles. This can suggest a period of time spent wearing a special outfit or uniform.

Nine of Circles - Unicorn
The future.

This can indicate that the questioner is psychic or that he will soon develop psychic powers. Otherwise, it counsels that thought will be needed when planning the long term future, also that the questioner needs to look beyond his immediate situation and to make long term plans.

The Suit of Numbers

Ace of Numbers - Entering
Door.
This is the doorway to new opportunities.

Two of Numbers - Sword
Dilemma.
A sword has two sharp edges and it can cut both ways, so this suggests that a choice will have to be made between two possible actions.

Three of Numbers - Earth
Land.
This suggests that new land will soon become important to the questioner. This may be in the form of living in a new environment, which would be in the country rather than the town. Alternatively, the questioner may buy or rent land (not property) for some purpose.

Four of Numbers - Lute
Music.
A time to rest and relax, to enjoy parties and celebrations and to listen to music. Work should be set aside for a while, as a break is needed. In some cases, the questioner might take up music as a hobby or even as a career.

Five of Numbers - House
Building.
This suggests a change of address. This may be a temporary arrangement, due to visiting friends or even staying in hospital. A particular building may become familiar to the questioner through a change in his place of work. Alternatively, the questioner might move house or business premises. If this tile is close by the Ace or Three of Numbers, an important move is definitely on the way.

Six of Numbers - Fire
Danger.

There are two distinct meanings to this tile. The best is that intelligence, inspiration and a stroke of genius are on the way, and it can also indicate the use of intelligence to solve a tricky problem. However, the alternative is a warning of danger, especially if the Nine of Bamboo is anywhere close by.

Seven of Numbers - Seven stars
Hope.

This is an exact duplicate of the Star card in the Tarot deck. When this card appears, the outlook is good and there is much to hope for. The questioner will use his creative imagination and writing talents, but he must ensure that his efforts come to fruition.

Eight of Numbers - Knot
Difficulties.

If this tile turns up in the center of the spread, it denotes anxiety and tension. If close to the Two of Bamboo, it suggests marriage or some other kind of beneficial relationship. If close to the Two of Numbers, it may indicate divorce, leaving a job, or some other means of cutting ties.

Nine of Numbers - Heaven
Temple.

On its own, this tile denotes a time of achievement and an increase in spiritual and psychic abilities. It can suggest an interest in religion, philosophy or ancient wisdom, and this is especially so if this tile is found in the east row. In other terms, when close to the Five of Numbers, it brings a wedding, and when close to the Six of Bamboo, it signifies long distance travel.

The Honors

These link with many of the other divinations in this book, because they hark back to the roots of Chinese divination and philosophical thought. Some Chinese people refer to these tiles as Dragons.

East - The Questioner

Tiles that are close to this one refer directly to the questioner and not to anything that others may do for him or against him. The tile can relate to success, achievement and advancement, but if it is next to the West tile, it represents partnership matters rather than "stand alone" matters.

South - Reward

In all Chinese divinations, the south is where good things come from. In the cold areas of northern China, the south represents the place where the sun shines, and therefore indicates good crops, food for animals and plenty of everything. The tile represents success, fame and good fortune, and indicates that any question will be answered favorably.

West - Objective

This tile gives an either/or answer. When difficult tiles surround it, or if it is found in the north area of the spread, it is not particularly fortunate. If it is in the west and close to good tiles, things should go well. If it is in the east, partnership matters will become important to the questioner.

North - Obstacles

In Chinese divinations, the wet and icy north is where trouble comes from. Bad weather can cause disaster to a rural nation. It is actually better for this tile to appear in the north of the spread, as this indicates that some preparation can be made in order to alleviate future problems. Perhaps the questioner has already taken out insurance against a rainy day. If the tile appears in the south, the problems will soon be solved. This tile also represents hardship, obstacles and conflicts with those who are in positions of authority.

Green - Commence
Proceed.

Time to make a start on a new enterprise or to go ahead with plans.

Red - Center
Success.

This suggests that the questioner will achieve his ambition. It denotes an arrow striking a target. It is especially good if found in the center of the spread.

White - The Unknown

This is a blank tile, and it indicates an unknown element in one's life, or a task that has not yet been completed. If combined with the Two of Circles, documents and letters need to be attended to. If it appears close to a Guardian tile or if more than one white tile appears, the questioner has psychic powers.

The Guardians

These tiles are very close to playing and the Major Arcana in a deck of Tarot cards. They are rarely used in the game of Mah Jong, just as the Joker is often discarded in playing cards. They are used, however, in Mah Jong readings. The red tiles represent plants and the blue tiles represent seasons.

Plum Blossom - Love.

A difficult relationship will improve. If the questioner is lonely, love will soon come along. Happiness in love is assured.

Orchid - Elegance.

If a daughter is sick or worried, she will soon feel better. Otherwise, it suggests that lost items of value to the questioner will be returned or found.

Chrysanthemum - Maturity.

This brings good news to older women, including love, prosperity, wellbeing, peace, contentment, a holiday or a pleasant break.

Bamboo - Wisdom.

Success and good news. If the questioner is taking an examination or completing a course, he will be pleased with the results. Good news may come in the post or by phone, especially when a Bamboo tile is close by.

Spring - Tolerance.

This card suggests that patience will be needed. In matters of love, nothing will come right overnight, and it will take time before the questioner gets what he wants. In business or gambling, the advice is to play things safe.

Summer - Fertility.

The questioner needs to make an effort in order to get results, and if he does this he will surely win out. This card indicates recovery from anxiety, mental illness and even from addictions. (We see drugs as a modern phenomenon, but opium addiction has been known in China for centuries).

Autumn - Promotion.

This is a time of harvest and reward for hard work. The questioner's health should be good, but he needs to take more exercise. Prosperity is on the way, as are a happy marriage and the birth of children into the family circle.

Winter - Prudence.

Don't waste time or allow time to drift away. If there is nothing else of interest going on, the Questioner should study something, practice and improve his talents. This might suggest taking up a sport or a musical hobby in order to stretch the mind and body.

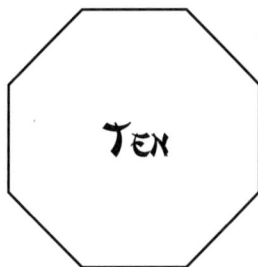

TEN

The Four Pillars of Destiny

Similarities to western astrology - further information - the Four Pillars in action - table of the seasons & months

The "Four Pillars of Destiny" system (also known as the Four Emperors), is very well known to Chinese fortune-tellers, but it is practically unheard of in the west. It is a very advanced form of what one could loosely call "astrology", although it would be better described as erecting a chart from a special form of calendar or almanac. The original system started out as the study of the stars, but some early emperors blocked real astrology, so this spin-off method was slowly developed and used in its place.

This system is, unfortunately, so complicated that you may not make much headway with it. I honestly think I could only get this across properly in person during a weekend workshop session, but I have included the system in this book because it just wouldn't be complete without it. I have confined the information to the absolute basics. If nothing else, it will show you what the Four Pillars of Destiny is about.

Similarities to western astrology

The closest thing that the Four Pillar system resembles for us in the west is the technique of weighting in western astrology. By this I mean examining a natal chart to see how many planets and angles are in signs of Fire, Earth, Air or Water, and assessing the character of a person based on that result. An abundance of one element obviously enhances that side of the person's character, while a lack of an element means that the subject has difficulty with that side of life. For example, in western astrology, a person whose chart emphases the element of Earth is sensible, practical and capable, but when Earth is absent from a chart, the subject may lack a sense of proportion and he would not wish to work with his hands. The Chinese assess a Four Pillar chart in much the same way, by measuring the number of items in the five elements of Wood, Fire, Earth, Metal and Water, and then assessing the balance between the elements. They develop this in a way that goes on to show how these elements work to benefit each other, or to destroy each other. The same rules that appear in Feng Shui appear here, and the nearest equivalent to this would be the kind of aspects in western astrology that fight against each other.

When the elements follow one another in their proper order (Wood, Fire, Earth, Metal, Water), they are creative or constructive. Any element that is two away from another is considered to be destructive. For instance, an abundance of Wood, followed by Earth is considered difficult.

The Four Pillar charts can be used in what western astrologers call synastry, which means looking at the charts of two people to see how they will get along with each other. This is where the weighting really come into its own, because a person who is predominantly Water will not get on well with someone who is predominantly Earth. Much the same goes for western astrology, where an intellectual air type would have a very hard time understanding a predominantly emotional Water type; or a practical Earth type would have a hard time understanding the speedy and intuitive Fire type.

Finally, there is a method of progressing these charts to show how various stages of one's life will work out.

Sources of further information

I have found two books on this subject but I was not impressed with either of them and have not listed them. In the meantime, my husband, Jan, took the trouble to surf his beloved Internet, and discovered some software that calculated the Four Pillars of Destiny. We purchased the software and I then painstakingly checked this out against the calculations in my two Chinese books and with reference to my own Chinese almanac. (I actually taught myself to read the Chinese characters while writing this book!) As far as I can tell, the software is accurate, but it seems to have a few bugs in it. For example, the program suggests that the user can elect to use a lunar or a solar calendar, but when trying these, Jan and I found they gave exactly the same results. The program also offers the user the opportunity of using local time or Beijing time, but when we tried this we discovered either method only came up with the information for local time. If you treat yourself to this software, I suggest that you stick to lunar time and either leave the local time as it is or make the adjustment yourself to your own birth hour, to fit Beijing time. The instructions for this adjustment are in the chapter on Chinese astrology.

The Four Pillars in action

So after all this preamble, the chart that one arrives at ends up looking like the table below. This chart is based on Beijing time.

	Hour	Day	Month	Year
Stem	Metal +	Fire -	Metal +	Water -
Branch	Dragon	Goat	Monkey	Goat
Branch element	Earth +	Earth -	Metal +	Earth -

The top row

The top row simply shows what the four columns refer to. The order is always the same, i.e. Hour, Day, Month, Year.

The second row

This shows the elements that were in operation during the Hour, Day, Month and Year of the person's birth. You may remember from the chapter on astrology that the elements run for two years

at a time, that the first year is Yang and the second is Yin. The plus
and minus signs beside each element show whether the element in
question is in its Yang or Yin phase.

The third row

This is the animal sign for that particular Hour, Day etc. It is
the animal that makes the element above it Yang or Yin. The following list shows the Yang/Yin order:

Rat	Yang
Ox	Yin
Tiger	Yang
Rabbit	Yin
Dragon	Yang
Snake	Yin
Horse	Yang
Goat	Yin
Monkey	Yang
Rooster	Yin
Dog	Yang
Pig	Yin

The fourth row

Now we attach each animal sign to its corresponding Month
in the monthly chart, and list the element and its Yang or Yin symbol.

A table of the seasons and the months

Spring			Summer		
Feb	Mar	Apr	May	Jun	Jul
Wood	Wood	Earth	Fire	Fire	Earth
Tiger	Rabbit	Dragon	Snake	Horse	Goat
Yang	Yin	Yang	Yin	Yang	Yin
Autumn			**Winter**		
Aug	Sep	Oct	Nov	Dec	Jan
Metal	Metal	Earth	Water	Water	Earth
Monkey	Rooster	Dog	Pig	Rat	Ox
Yang	Yin	Yang	Yin	Yang	Yin

In the sample chart shown earlier in this chapter, the person was born during the year of the Water Goat. The month that the Goat appears in is attached to Earth, so the third row reads Earth. The month, day and hour are treated in exactly the same way; that is the actual animal and element that ruled at the time, and its association with the animal month.

You will notice that every third month is attached to the element of Earth. Each of the animals remains Yang or Yin, as they do in every other aspect of Chinese astrology. The elements each have a Yang or Yin month attached to them, and the doubled elements of Fire and Water start with a Yin month.

This return to Earth is a very Chinese concept. A person may travel in some direction or other, but he eventually returns to the centre. The sun and stars themselves may appear to move from one part of the sky to another, depending upon the time of day or the time of year, but they always return at some point. China was considered to be the "middle kingdom", the centre of the civilized world and everything that went on around it and returned to it.

If you find yourself fascinated by all this, I suggest that you try and find a Chinese teacher who can show you the method in detail. Believe me, the material that I have space for in this chapter is only the start of the system - it goes much further than this!

Eleven

The Lo Shu or Nine Star Ki

Overview - the Lo Shu Magic Square - basic numerology - your year number - table of year numbers - your month number - table of month numbers - character reading - taking things further - the Key Magic Square - the system in action - worth remembering - reading the future - monthly predictions - interpreting the Magic Square Houses

When I started researching this book, I was open-minded about all the systems I intended to use, but after doing the required research, this divination is definitely my favorite.

The Lo Shu is also known as the Lo Map and the Nine Star Ki. The term "Nine Star Ki" has caught on in the west, but this is actually a Japanese name; so, if you mention this to someone from China they will look blank, but the moment you say Lo Shu, they will know exactly what you are talking about. So, for the purposes of this very Chinese book, we will stick to the name Lo Shu. The Lo Shu is a numerology system that is used for character reading, prediction and also for Feng Shui.

Overview

The thinking behind the Lo Shu is obvious to those who have been born and brought up in China, in much the same way that Westerners immediately understand our familiar signs of the zodiac. For example, you don't have to be an astrologer to know that

Taureans are stubborn and that Scorpios have a sting in their tails. Thus, in exactly the same way, if you describe your lover as being a Metal person to a Chinese friend, they will immediately know that your lover is hard to influence or to dictate to.

The challenge for me in this chapter is to ignore all those things that make immediate sense to an Oriental person and to make the subject accessible to Westerners. However, I do go into the symbolism and the details later on, for those of you who want a glimpse at what is behind it all. As always, if this chapter fires your interest in the Lo Shu, I suggest that you go on to read other books about it. If you want to do this, look for books on Nine Star Ki, Feng Shui and Feng Shui astrology, as they all usually have something to say about the Lo Shu.

The Lo Shu Magic Square

The central feature of the Lo Shu system is something called the Magic Square. If you have read through the chapter on Feng Shui, you will have already met up with the Magic Square. In Feng Shui, the Magic Square is used to define areas of your house or place of work that relate to career, health, relationships and so forth. You can discover more about this Magic Square and how the same connections that apply to your house,

4	9	2
3	5	7
8	1	6

Magic Square

also apply to travel directions and your character, in the advanced section at the end of this chapter.

Basic numerology

The following text would make any Oriental person weep, because I have dispensed with the poetry and symbolism, but for the likes of you and I, this now becomes easy to work out and to understand. Having said this, you will still need to apply yourself a little, if only to look up a few dates and numbers and to discover their meanings. To give you even more help, I have given the various sections logical names that make the system easy to deal with.

Once you have done the figure work, you can check out your own character traits, as well as those of friends and loved ones.

How to find your year number

To locate your year number, find your year of birth in the chart below, then track upwards to the number directly above the column that contains your birth year.

The only complication is that the Chinese year begins on the 4th of February. The early Chinese scholars and emperors settled on this date because it was easier for them to work with, than the "floating" dates that start each year at the time of the new moon, when the New Year is formally celebrated.

Thus, if you happen to have been born between the 1st of January and the 4th of February, you must count your year as the previous one. A good example is my husband, Jan, whose birthday is the 3rd of February 1944. Jan counts his "year" as 1943.

There is one further point to watch for; people born at the "cusp" of the new year (roughly the first week of February) tend to show some characteristics from both the previous and current years, in a kind of overlap situation. This arises in western astrology as well, and "cuspy" people should study both interpretations in order to gain a more complete understanding of themselves. Jan would like to adopt the best bits from each year and leave out the rest, but I have told him not to push weird Aquarian logic too far!

Example: President Bill Clinton was born on 19th August 1946, so his year number is 9.

Year Numbers 1901 - 2017

9	8	7	6	5	4	3	2	1
1901	1902	1903	1904	1905	1906	1907	1908	1909
1910	1911	1912	1913	1914	1915	1916	1917	1918
1919	1920	1921	1922	1923	1924	1925	1926	1927
1928	1929	1930	1931	1932	1933	1934	1935	1936
1937	1938	1939	1940	1941	1942	1943	1944	1945

1946	1947	1948	1949	1950	1951	1952	1953	1954
1955	1956	1957	1958	1959	1960	1961	1962	1963
1964	1965	1966	1967	1968	1969	1970	1971	1972
1973	1974	1975	1976	1977	1978	1979	1980	1981
1982	1983	1984	1985	1986	1987	1988	1989	1990
1991	1992	1993	1994	1995	1996	1997	1998	1999
2000	2001	2002	2003	2004	2005	2006	2007	2008
2009	2010	2011	2012	2013	2014	2015	2016	2017

How to find your month number

The illustration below shows all the year numbers at the top of the three columns.

First, make a mental note of your YEAR NUMBER (above).

Now track down the left-hand column (below) to find your birthday.

Finally, track along to the number that is in the column containing your YEAR NUMBER.

Example: President Bill Clinton's birthday is the 19th of August; his year number is 9; his year number is in the third column heading, so his month number (third column) is 8.

Birth Date	1,4,7	5,2,8	3,6,9
4 February to 5 March	8	2	5
6 March to 5 April	7	1	4
6 April to 5 May	6	9	3
6 May to 5 June	5	8	2
6 June to 7 July	4	7	1
8 July to 7 August	3	6	9
8 August to 7 September	2	5	8
8 September to 8 October	1	4	7
9 October to 7 November	9	3	6
8 November to 7 December	8	2	5
8 December to 5 January	7	1	4
6 January to 3 February	6	9	3

At this point, it is well worth noting down your YEAR NUM-
BER and your MONTH NUMBER on a piece of paper, because you
will be using both these numbers again a little later on.

Character reading

For the time being, I suggest that you look up your year number and your month numbers in the following section on the personality traits of each number. This will give you something useful,
without having to go into the real complications of the subject. So
to clarify matters, if you happen to have Number Five as your year
number, read through the interpretation for that number, and if your
month number is Number Eight, simply read through the interpretation for that number. Doing this will give you as good an indication
as any of the system in action.

If you decide that you want to take a deeper interest in the Lo
Shu and its connection to the I Ching, you will have to look for
other books that give you more detail; this book can only go so far
without turning into an immense tome! The full system gives a similar
kind of character reading to basic western astrology birth-chart reading, although the roots and the technique are quite different. If you
try to gain a really deep understanding of the character of each trigram of the I Ching, you will then be able to attach each one to the
numbers in the Lo Shu and gain more insight into the personality of
the person you want to study.

It is, of course, possible to progress the system through the
various "houses" in the Lo Shu square, in order to check out the
trends and likely events during a specific period of time. This means
moving the numbers around in the square according to the date and
time that you want to study, which might for example, be some time
during the coming year. This technique allows an expert to study
the events that are likely to be in evidence at any time during a
client's life. If you are keen to move on to this level, look for good
books on the Nine Star Ki or Lo Shu system.

The following text shows you the personality traits of each of the numbers, so once you have found your month and year number, look them up and see how they fit you and your loved ones.

Number One

Being primarily a western astrologer, I can't help noticing that there is a connection between the signs of Scorpio and to a lesser extent Libra with the number one type. Read on and you will soon see what I mean.

Personality

This person is a deep thinker who can brood over imagined insults. He may have strange religious or political views, and if he gets himself into a position of real power, he can wreak havoc, although some Number One types, like Nelson Mandela, can be inspired leaders. Some are extremely restless and unsettled, following one idea after another, or moving from one place to another in search of something that eludes them.

Relationships

Where love relationships are concerned, sex is all-important to the One type. Males in particular may confuse sex with love and they may accuse a partner who doesn't want sex all the time of not loving them enough. These people learn by experience though, and they improve with age.

Career

Number One people are not really attracted to business and they are not team players, neither can they cope with heavy manual work. They are best suited to careers that allow them to express their inner world, such as the arts or literature. They need work that calls upon their reserves of self-motivation and self-discipline, and that gives them an opportunity to use their intellect. Therefore work in some form of research, computer programming, some forms of engineering, writing, printing, silk-screening, design, illustrating or music might suit these types. Number One people may be interested in health as a sideline, especially alternative therapies such as aromatherapy, massage or herbalism. Watery jobs such as fishing and the oil industry might attract. These people are good at keeping records and allocating stock, inventory and resources.

Health

Their physical weak spots are similar to those of Libra and Scorpio, these being the kidneys, bladder, lower spine and reproductive organs. They should avoid too much salt or sugar and they should wrap up warmly in bad weather.

Nutshells

Lucky numbers: 6 and 7.

Fairly lucky numbers: 3 and 4.

Neutral number: 1.

Best color: White, or silver.

Element: Water.

Number Two

There is something of Cancer with a touch of the Mercury ruled signs of Gemini or Virgo about this personality, as you will see when you read the following text.

Personality

Whatever the gender, these subjects are motherly personalities who take care of all those around them. They are excellent hosts and caterers, ensuring that their guests always have plenty to eat and drink. Number Two personalities make excellent organizers, and some like to teach. They need to be part of a family or the kind of working group that feels like a family, because if they are alone for too long they become depressed. Their main fault is fussiness and too much attendance to detail. These people enjoy the countryside and they should get out into it from time to time as a kind of balm for their nerves.

Relationships

Number two types have the ability to attract the opposite sex quite easily, but potential partners may mistake their motives and see them as sex-objects rather than the loving family people they really are. When in a relationship, their fussiness or obsessive behavior can cause problems.

Career

In business, they work well under direction and as part of a team. They love to work in fields that help others or that provide for the needs of others, like nursing, catering, shop keeping (especially bakeries and grocery shops), also farming. Many Number Twos love dealing with antiques and gifts. Others lean towards the construction industry or civil engineering.

Health

Their weak spots are their digestive organs, spleen, pancreas and stomach. They need a sensible diet without too much sugar, alcohol or coffee. The lymph system can become clogged, so gentle exercise, massage or aromatherapy work wonders for them.

Nutshells

Lucky numbers: 5,8 and 9.

Fairly lucky numbers: 6 and 7.

Neutral number: 2.

Best color: Black or dark blue.

Element: Earth

Number Three

Western astrologers will find number three types similar to the fire sign of Sagittarius with a touch of Aries as well.

Personality

These people are courageous and idealistic, and they can be a little too frank in their opinions. They are vigorous and energetic and they sometimes forget that not everyone else has their level of enthusiasm or energy. They love to come up with great ideas and they often have a number of projects on the go at once, but their dislike of detail means that their projects may not come to much in the long run. These ebullient folk are great fun at a party and they are extremely easy to like, but too much of their company can overwhelm more sensitive souls. Even when they offend others, their ability to talk their way out of trouble or to make others laugh is a great help to them. These people can be very much into their own appearance, buying clothes, cosmetics and visiting the beauty parlor as often as they can afford.

Number Three people don't take kindly to being restricted. Much of this seems to stem from their childhood, where one or both of their parents tried to keep them down. In later life, they can explode in temper if frustrated. An uncaring or envious mother can undermine their confidence, giving them an insecure side to their nature, which is hidden by their brash outer manner. Sometimes the father is a bully and the mother is not strong enough to stand up to him. One survey has turned up the fact that number three women tend to be sexually abused in childhood.

Relationships

Where love relationships are concerned, they seem to want it all. They need an intense relationship with plenty of emotion, sex and touching. They seek an exciting partner. However, they also need their freedom, which can cause the breakdown of one settled relationship after another.

Career

Number Three people need careers that allow them to use their inventive minds. Modern industries such as computer programming and inventions for the Internet would appeal to them. They are innovative and they have the kind of mind that takes well to engineering, the electronics industry or the construction industry. They may work in the media, either on the technical side or as personalities. Writing and teaching might appeal. If in an organization, they need to be allowed to give their creativity and inventiveness free rein. They can see the big picture but they don't always know how to make it happen. When under intense pressure, they blow a fuse and either have a major row or quietly quit the job and find another.

Health

Traditionally, their weak spots are the liver and the gall bladder, so fatty foods and alcohol are not good for them. Unfortunately, this personality often does drink too much. The muscles, ligaments and tendons can also suffer, so a balance between gentle exercise and rest is required.

Nutshells
Lucky numbers: 1 and 4.
Fairly lucky number: 9.
Neutral number: 3.
Best color: Bright green.
Element: Wood

Number Four

To western astrologers, the Number Four personality is amazingly close to that of Aquarius, complete with the Aquarian's direct, penetrating gaze and all.

Personality

Number Four people tend to look cool and calm and their stubborn, determined, and independent nature gives them an appearance of being in control at all times. However, this is only superficial, because they can be quite tense and vulnerable inside, breaking out into moody, stubborn behavior when under intense pressure. They can see things clearly, they don't lack common sense and they know how to convince or influence others. Forward looking and innovative, these people are often ahead of their time. However, they are also sensitive to what is going on around them and they can make a great success of things when they get the timing right. They can't handle too many things at once, so they are best when working on a specific project and at their own pace. They sometimes leave things to the last minute, hence becoming labeled as procrastinators. If they are required to chop and change midstream, they become quite het up. The natural honesty of the Number Four type means that they put their trust in others far too easily, expecting them to have the same high standards of decency as themselves. They love music, and some enjoy art and literature as well.

Relationships

In love, they are true romantics. Their pleasant nature and arresting eyes make it easy for them to attract potential lovers, but they are extremely choosy about who they decide to make their own. Even when a relationship does not work out too well, they try to stick it out and to put things right. If all else fails, they keep the relationship going, while looking around for someone new. They can be attracted to the wrong person for financial reasons.

Career

These people do well in any career that requires mental agility, intelligence, patience and inventiveness. Dress design, politics, the arts and sports may attract, but it is in the field of inventions, engineering and computing that they really excel. They are happiest when employed by someone who appreciates them. They may not have the vision of some of the signs, but they can take a project and really make it work, improving it beyond the belief of those who thought it up in the first place. Number Four people must guard against frittering money away once they have it, so a good savings scheme is a must for these folk.

Health

Like the Number Three type, these people should take care of their livers and gall bladders. So, fatty food and alcohol should be restricted. Any gentle exercise that moves them around is good for them; jogging, golf, cycling, walking and swimming are recommended.

Nutshells

Lucky numbers: 1 and 3.

Fairly lucky number: 9.

Neutral number: 4.

Best color: Rich, dark green.

Element: Wood

Number Five

To western astrologers, this number links with the sign of Leo.

Personality

These charismatic people love to be at the center of things, and they often influence those around them in a positive manner. They tend to be the leaders in any situation, whether at home or at work, and they have to guard against being leaned upon too much.

They can be irritable, impatient and sometimes too blunt and inflexible. This trait can result in them making enemies unnecessarily, which is a shame because they are actually decent, honest and loyal. Number Five people have lives that reach very high and very low, and their fate and fortune can fluctuate wildly at times. When down, their determination and ability to work hard brings them back up again, but they must guard against sitting back and allowing things to slide back down again. Whatever their circumstances, they have an aura of success and confidence that encourages others to put their trust in them. To some extent, this is only an outer shield, because they are quite insecure and vulnerable inside; it is often only their loved ones who can see this side of their personality.

Relationships

Number Five people can attract lovers easily and they are wonderful lovers themselves, but their moodiness and occasional fits of depression can make them hard to live with. They do somehow manage to find themselves in love triangles and they can divorce, remarry and gain stepchildren as a result.

Career

Careers for Number Five types include selling and marketing or running their own businesses. Some work in the media or as military leaders. Politics attract some, due to their love of being at the heart of important matters, while others turn the same social urge towards running a hotel or restaurant or a social club.

Health

Health concerns are quite varied with the pancreas being a potential area to watch, with blood sugar problems high on the list, leading to heart disease and diabetes. Sometimes high blood pressure, tumors and cysts can be a problem. Also depression.

Nutshells

Lucky numbers: 2, 8 and 9.

Fairly lucky numbers: 6 and 7.

Neutral number: 5.

Best color: Yellow.

Element: Earth.

Number Six

This number links best with the sign of Capricorn, with some Aries thrown in.

Personality

These people have strong personalities and they exhibit great leadership qualities. Sometimes this shows itself in the sense of being a military leader or business head, but in other contexts, this type becomes a strong and reliable father figure. These people like to make provision for their families, and this extends to their siblings as well as their spouses and children. These people are orderly, highly responsible and often very moral. Their lack of flexibility or ability to allow for the weaknesses of others can make them unpopular. They do have weaknesses, but these are well concealed. If they fail in an enterprise, they can become quite paralyzed for a while, doing nothing much at all until something else inspires them. Sometimes their standards are too high, even for themselves and certainly for others, making them critical and inwardly self-critical. These hardworking types can become rich and powerful in almost any sphere of action and some do very well in sporting and competitive activities. They take care of those who are under them.

Relationships

Needless to say, relationship matters can be their downfall because they may simply not have the time and energy to devote to these. Both sexes are great achievers and they may take on more than they can handle. Either sex can become bullies. However, if they marry later in life, once they have made their pile, they can relax back, enjoy home and family life, and become very caring lovers.

Career

Careers that allow them to become leaders are the obvious ones for Number Six people, therefore the military, the police, big business and also the church would appeal. In some cases the law or transport might apply, but also politics and local government work.

Health

Health matters affect the lungs, but skin problems and headaches are also possible, as are heart problems and broken bones due to playing rough sports. Inner tension can lead to high blood pressure or headaches.

Nutshells

Lucky numbers: 2, 5, 7 and 8.

Fairly lucky number: 1.

Neutral number: 6.

Best color: White.

Element: Metal.

Number Seven

These attractive, amusing and intelligent people can be similar to a combination of Libra and Gemini or Pisces in western astrology.

Personality

Number Seven people enjoy the good life and they love to dine out, have nice holidays and buy good clothes and other possessions. They can be great fun, with outgoing and cheerful natures, but there is a certain self-indulgence to them and an assumption that the world owes them a living. They usually manage to find the money they need to finance their lifestyle. These people manage to say the right thing at the right time to the right people, and they can delight an audience with their wit and repartee. They dislike confrontation and arguments, and they may be too insecure to stand up for themselves. Their innate sense of style can take them into the fields of fashion or entertainment, where their good looks and meticulously chosen outfits are set to impress others. These people often look younger than their years.

Relationships

They fall in love quite easily, but they can become bored and wish to move on fairly quickly, although quite often, they may not know how to say this. Many Number Seven types prefer to remain single, but if they do marry, the odds are against them being faithful or sticking with the same partner.

Career

Oddly enough, despite the pleasure loving and apparently lighthearted nature of the Number Seven personalities, they often work in fields that require a good deal of financial acumen and a strong sense of responsibility. These may include banking, savings and loans specialists, accountants, stock-controllers, mortgage brokers and so on. More obviously, the entertainment industry, arranging sports fixtures, public relations or running a smart restaurant, hotel or club. Lecturing and even mildly medical or therapeutic fields might appeal.

Health

The health weak spots are the colon, bowels and also the chest and breasts. The hips and cranium are susceptible to injury.

Nutshells

Lucky numbers: 2,5,6 and 8.

Fairly lucky number: 1.

Neutral number: 7.

Best color: Red.

Element: Metal

Number Eight

To a western astrologer, this number type is a bit like Taurus with some Scorpio and Capricorn thrown in.

Personality

These people are hard workers whose meticulous attention to detail insures that all their tasks are properly performed, although sometimes this attention to detail makes them lose sight of the larger picture. Slow, thorough, single minded and determined, these people get the job done. If their business ventures fail or if they lose their money, they are able work their way back up and to make a second or even a third fortune later in life. These folk move slowly and their calm exterior gives confidence to others. They sometimes find it hard to make a decision and they can lose faith in themselves at times of stress. Their calm exterior and apparent lack of emotion can lead them into counseling careers, and their strong moral views can lead them into becoming active in human rights or matters of ecology. The conservative Number Eight types don't accept change readily.

Relationships

In love relationships they are the type who enjoy a quiet and stress free family life. These people can be a great support to their loved ones, but they need the security of a loving and supportive marriage in order to be happy.

Career

Career choices might include working any kind of service industry, and also manufacturing, farming, haulage and the provision of goods. Some will be drawn to the police, civil service or banking, while others prefer to work in the fields of beauty, hair and cosmetics.

Health

Health areas to be watched are rheumatic aches and pains, obesity, constipation, trouble with the legs or with the sinus, and also depression and hypochondria.

Nutshells

Lucky numbers: 2, 5 and 9.

Fairly lucky numbers: 6 and 7.

Neutral number: 8.

Best color: White.

Element: Earth.

Number Nine

The Number Nine person to a western astrologer is like a combination of any or all the mutable signs of Gemini, Virgo, Sagittarius and Pisces.

Personality

These charismatic people enjoy the limelight and they get noticed wherever they are. They are great communicators who can inspire others and guide them through troubled times. They may be excellent salespeople and they can promote themselves well. Their strong sense of right may lead them into some form of religious leadership, and they can become the spokesperson for a group. Others among the Number Nine group are just as happy to be one of a crowd. They are honest, they don't carry grudges and they may trust others a little too much, because they don't understand hidden agendas or ulterior motives. These warm, passionate people are not especially competitive, but their attractive appearance, communications skill and ability to lift the spirits of others can take them far. There is a streak of vanity among Number Nine folk and they love to have the best clothes, a nice home and an impressive car to ride around in. They dislike bad manners and scruffy or sloppy people. They may expect too much of others and be a little disappointed, but in business or relationships, if something doesn't work out, they move on fairly easily.

Relationships

In love relationships, their romantic soul means that they express emotion well. They draw others to them quite easily, but they need to develop some discrimination about their choice of partner. They can become arrogant and fickle, but they stick to a lover while the affair is current, then move on and put the whole thing behind them. Adaptability is the name of the game for Number Nine folk, whether in work, relationships or life in general.

Career

Career options might include the entertainment industry, the media or also customer relations, selling, public relations and marketing. Politics might appeal, as would the media, journalism and photography. Team building, networking, socializing and conducting an orchestra could be appropriate. Basically any job that requires the Number Nine person to think on his feet and to cope with a number of different things at once. Variety is the spice of life in any job for this type.

Health

It would be sensible to balance the outgoing, active nature of this group by including any form of relaxation that appeals, be it meditation, reading, fishing or other non-strenuous hobbies. The heart, intestines and blood circulation are areas to watch.

Nutshells

Lucky numbers: 3 and 4.

Fairly lucky numbers: 2, 8 and 9.

Neutral number: 9.

Best color: Dark wine red.

Element: Fire.

TAKING THINGS FURTHER

As with many chapters in this book, you now have the option of leaving the subject at this point, or of taking it a stage further. If you find yourself becoming ever more fascinated by the Lo Shu, look around in shops and on the Internet for books on the Nine Star Ki, Chinese Astrology, Feng Shui astrology and the I Ching. All these systems mix and blend with each other, so if you want to become an expert in any one of them, you will need to study them all. For the moment, let us take things just one step further.

Back to the Magic Square

We have already seen the Magic Square in action, in the chapter on Feng Shui in the context of property and land, and now it appears again for the purposes of divination. We can use the Magic Square for character reading, prediction and also for advice on travel and location.

The Magic Square is called "magic" because the numbers in the square always add up to fifteen, horizontally, vertically or diagonally.

4	9	2
3	5	7
8	1	6

Key Magic Square

The Magic Square that rules this system is the same as the one in the chapter on Feng Shui. For the purposes of the Lo Shu, I call that particular Magic Square the Key Magic Square.

The Key Magic Square

Now you must look at a further nine Magic Squares - illustrated below - and follow my instructions very carefully. It would be a good idea to photocopy this chapter so that you can scribble directly on to the diagrams while you are experimenting with the system.

There will come a point on at least one occasion where you want to refer back to one or another of the Squares, so I have awarded them western names to prevent you from getting lost.

The names I have chosen are from the international alphabet used by airline pilots and police forces around the world.

Read through the instructions below, then work through the examples, and you will see that the system is far easier than it first appears. When you get the hang of it, you will be able to do it surprisingly quickly.

The system in action

1. Look at the piece of paper on which you have noted down your Year and Month Numbers.
2. Look at the nine Magic Squares below, and find the one that has the number corresponding to your Month Number in the middle of the square.

3.   Look at the square and make a note of the position of your Year Number (i.e. it may be above, below, left, right or diagonal).

4.   Look at the KEY MAGIC SQUARE, note the number that is in the same position that your Year Number falls in, and then note down the cross-referenced number that you find there.

Now you will have three numbers to cope with. The first is your Month Number, the second is your Year Number and the third is your Magic Square number.

Let us work through this, using Bill Clinton as an example:

1.   You may remember that Bill Clinton's Year Number is 9 and his Month Number is 8.

2.   The Magic Square that has Bill's Month Number in the center is Magic Square Bravo.

3.   In Magic Square Bravo, Bill's Year Number falls in the lower right hand corner.

4.   Now we look at the Key Magic Square and note the number in that same lower right hand corner.

5.   The lower right hand corner of the Key Magic Square is 6.

Thus the whole sequence for Bill Clinton is as follows:
Bill Clinton's Year Number is: 9
Bill Clinton's Month Number is: 8
Bill Clinton's Magic Square number is: 6
Thus, Bill's numbers are expressed as: 9.8.6.

Once you have worked out your own number combination, refer back to the number interpretations earlier in this chapter and see how the different facets of your personality blend with each other.

8	4	6
7	9	2
3	5	1

Alpha

7	3	5
6	8	1
2	4	9

Bravo

6	2	4
5	7	9
1	3	8

Charlie

5	1	3
4	6	8
9	2	7

Delta

4	9	2
3	5	7
8	1	6

Echo

3	8	1
2	4	6
7	9	5

Foxtrot

2	7	9
1	3	5
6	8	4

Golf

1	6	8
9	2	4
5	7	3

Hotel

9	5	7
8	1	3
4	6	2

India

4	9	2
3	5	7
8	1	6

Key Magic Square

An important reminder!

Remember that it is your Month Number that goes in the center of the square!

A point worth making

The three number arrangement of the Lo Shu has a similar feeling to the combination of the sun sign, moon sign and ascendant in western astrology. This also shows where you and your loved ones are alike in nature and where you differ. For example, if you have one number in exactly the same place (i.e. the same Year Number, Month Number or Magic Square number) as someone else, there will be a rapport between you. Western astrologers can see the same effect when looking at two people who have similarities on their horoscope charts.

Predicting the future

You can discover what a particular year or a particular month will hold for you, by a system of number swapping. Detailed instructions follow, but the basic idea is to find the Lo Shu House that represents the year or the month that you want to know about.

This is mildly complicated, but if you follow the instructions carefully, you shouldn't have any real difficulty.

1. Write down your Year Number.

If you forgot to make a note of it, I have repeated the system here so that you can do it again without having to refer back through the book.

2. To locate your Year Number, look at the chart below and then track upwards to the number at the top of the column that your year falls in.

(The only complication is that the Chinese year begins on the 4th of February, so if you happen to have been born between the 1st of January and the 4th of February, you must count your year as the previous one.)

Year Numbers 1901 - 2017

9	8	7	6	5	4	3	2	1
1901	1902	1903	1904	1905	1906	1907	1908	1909
1910	1911	1912	1913	1914	1915	1916	1917	1918
1919	1920	1921	1922	1923	1924	1925	1926	1927
1928	1929	1930	1931	1932	1933	1934	1935	1936
1937	1938	1939	1940	1941	1942	1943	1944	1945
1946	1947	1948	1949	1950	1951	1952	1953	1954
1955	1956	1957	1958	1959	1960	1961	1962	1963
1964	1965	1966	1967	1968	1969	1970	1971	1972
1973	1974	1975	1976	1977	1978	1979	1980	1981
1982	1983	1984	1985	1986	1987	1988	1989	1990
1991	1992	1993	1994	1995	1996	1997	1998	1999
2000	2001	2002	2003	2004	2005	2006	2007	2008
2009	2010	2011	2012	2013	2014	2015	2016	2017
2018	2019	2020	2021	2022	2023			

3.   Now choose a year that you would like to examine and find its Year Number at the top of the table.

For instance, if you wanted to look at the situation in 2002, when you consult the table, you soon find that 2002 is a Number Seven year.

4.   Now look at all those named Squares (Alpha, Bravo etc.) and find the square that has the number for the year that you wish to examine in its middle.

Example: The Square for a Number Seven year is Charlie.

```
┌─────┬─────┬─────┐
│  6  │  2  │  4  │
├─────┼─────┼─────┤
│  5  │  7  │  9  │
├─────┼─────┼─────┤
│  1  │  3  │  8  │
└─────┴─────┴─────┘
      Charlie
```

5.   Now find the position of your own Year Number on this square.

Example: If your Year Number is Three, you will find this in the middle of the bottom row of the Charlie Square. This position is now called a "House".

```
┌─────┬─────┬─────┐
│  6  │  2  │  4  │
├─────┼─────┼─────┤
│  5  │  7  │  9  │
├─────┼─────┼─────┤
│  1  │  3  │  8  │
└─────┴─────┴─────┘
      Charlie
```

6.   Now find the same House (position) on the Key Magic Square.

In our example, the House for Year Number Three is at the middle of the bottom row of the Charlie Square.

```
┌─────┬─────┬─────┐
│  4  │  9  │  2  │
├─────┼─────┼─────┤
│  3  │  5  │  7  │
├─────┼─────┼─────┤
│  8  │  1  │  6  │
└─────┴─────┴─────┘
  Key Magic Square
```

The House in that position on the Key Magic Square contains the number One.

This means that a person born in a Number Seven Year who wants to investigate his prospects during 2002, which happens to be a Number Three Year, ends up with House Number One on the Key Magic Square.

The outlook for a Number One House year can now be looked up in the interpretations section a little further along in this chapter.

I will now go over the above instructions once again for you, in the hope that it sticks in your mind.

1. Find your year of birth and look up your Year Number.
2. Find the Year Number for the year you want to examine.
3. Find the named Magic Square (Alpha, Bravo etc.) that has the number for the year you wish to look into in its middle.
4. Find your own Year Number on that square and make a note of the House position.
5. Swap the House on the named Magic Square for the same House on the Key Magic Square.
6. Look up the prediction for the year in question.

Monthly predictions

Just as you can look at the prospects for a particular year, you can also do so for a particular month. I have repeated the list of months further on, to save you from having to flick back through this book.

1.   Find the number of the year that you are looking at.
2.   Find the Month Number for the year in question.

Do this by finding the column that has the Year Number at its head, and then check down the left-hand column until you find the month you want to look at.

Month Numbers

Year Numbers:	1,4,7	5,2,8	3,6,9
4 February to 5 March	8	2	5
6 March to 5 April	7	1	4
6 April to 5 May	6	9	3
6 May to 5 June	5	8	2
6 June to 7 July	4	7	1
8 July to 7 August	3	6	9
8 August to 7 September	2	5	8
8 September to 8 October	1	4	7
9 October to 7 November	9	3	6
8 November to 7 December	8	2	5
8 December to 5 January	7	1	4
6 January to 3 February	6	9	3

*3. Now find the named Square (Alpha, Bravo, etc.) that has
the Month Number in its middle.*

8	4	6		7	3	5		6	2	4
7	9	2		6	8	1		5	7	9
3	5	1		2	4	9		1	3	8
Alpha				**Bravo**				**Charlie**		

5	1	3		4	9	2		3	8	1
4	6	8		3	5	7		2	4	6
9	2	7		8	1	6		7	9	5
Delta				**Echo**				**Foxtrot**		

2	7	9		1	6	8		9	5	7
1	3	5		9	2	4		8	1	3
6	8	4		5	7	3		4	6	2
Golf				**Hotel**				**India**		

4.   Locate your own Year Number position on that Square to
      find the House (position).
5.   Swap this for the House Number on the Key Magic Square.

4	9	2
3	5	7
8	1	6
Key Magic Square		

6. Look up the House Number in the interpretation section that follows.

The interpretation of the Houses on the Key Magic Square

Once you have found the House Number for the year or the month you wish to examine, read the following interpretations. The Chinese will immediately understand the relevance of the Element, Season and Direction, and it is not particularly hard for Westerners who live in the Northern Hemisphere to follow this either. Water, Winter, North must necessarily represent a time of sitting things out, while other Elements, Seasons and directions are obviously more productive. People living in the Southern Hemisphere will have to remember that the interpretations are primarily orientated for the Northern Hemisphere, and adjust for that as necessary.

House One

Element: Water
Season: Winter
Direction: North

The dark, cold, wintry, northerly feeling of this House suggests a time of retreat and reflection. A rural image would suggest a time when nothing is growing, but when the farmer is planning what crops he will grow in the coming year.

In personal terms, this signifies a time of withdrawal when you spend time planning your future. Money may be in short supply and there is little opportunity for movement or expansion in your affairs. The connection with the element of Water suggests that this is a time to count what money you have and to make a sensible budget, or to arrange loans to see you over this period. You may push people away from you or withdraw emotionally from relationships or friendships. Caution, nervousness and even fear characterize this House, and you may suffer ill health during this period. You appear to be immobile, but you can take the time to plan and to set goals for yourself. The best course of action is to research or find the information you will need in preparation for whatever action and activity you will take in the next phase.

Your plans will depend upon your personal circumstances, but you could use this period to gain some kind of qualification or to study something that you have always wanted to know about. If you are stuck in a job that you don't find satisfying, this is not the time to make a change, because you would only find yourself in a similar situation somewhere else. If a relationship is dying, you will be aware of the fact but unable to improve things or to end it. A pleasant image might be of sitting by the fire, reading and resting, but a less pleasant one is of frustration at the lack of opportunities or of movement in your affairs. Your best course is to stay put and to do everything you can to learn what needs to be learned in order to improve your future prospects when times of change come around.

A positive side to this period is that your intuition will increase, and if you follow it you won't go too far wrong. This might be a time to take up some kind of alternative or stress relieving activity such as Tai Chi, yoga or meditation.

Water being a fluid, health problems associated with the blood, lymph drainage system, bladder and even the reproductive organs might arise at this time. Alcohol should be restricted. You should try to avoid environmental hazards, such as being caught in a flood, a blizzard or being on a mountain when mist and cloud descend. I guess even such things as your household gas appliances should be checked during this time. If you are living or working in a damp, cold environment, you should get away from this if you can.

If your own personal Year Number is 2,5,8 or 9 you will feel the restrictions and hardships more keenly.

House two

Element:	Earth
Season:	Early autumn
Direction:	Southwest

The Earth element and early autumn feel to this House suggest that a calm phase is in operation. A rural image might be of a farmer resting after the harvest is in.

You may find that nothing much changes during this period, and that your life is on a steady course. This is excellent if you are basically happy with your lifestyle, but if you are itching for changes, they won't come along during this phase. If you try to force change you will only irritate and possibly alienate others, as well as driving yourself crazy with frustration. This is a good time in which to clear up outstanding jobs, to clear out cupboards, make space for new things and to off-load tasks or even habits that are no longer necessary. Any developments that do occur will move quite slowly, but oddly enough, you may be able to change your address during this time.

Depending upon your personality type and your personal situation, you may become depressed about the lack of movement in your affairs, or you may boast about the happy state of your finances and your great lifestyle. The Earth element suggests that this may be a time to make minor improvements to your property or land, and to consolidate what you have rather than to expand.

Health problems are likely to be few, but swellings in the glands due to infection are possible, as are stones or fibroids forming somewhere in the body. Also the pancreas and spleen may give trouble. You will definitely need to take some exercise during this period.

If your own personal Year Number is 1, 3 or 4, you will find this period more difficult than others will.

House three

Element: Wood
Season: Spring
Direction: East

Everyone feels better when spring arrives, especially if the winter has been particularly cold, wet, dark and depressing. The sap rises in the trees and you feel that you are coming back to life again.

The rural image is an obvious one, as is the start of the farming year when plants sprout and animals give birth. Another image is that of the sunrise and the dawn of a new day.

On a personal level, ideas and inspiration flow and your creative juices are stimulated. Luck is with you now, and you can bring luck and inspiration to others. This is the time to get large enterprises off the ground and to break out of the mould. Anything can be initiated now, and this might include a move of house, the start of a relationship, opening a business or pushing for promotion at work. The only real danger is of moving so quickly that you neglect some vital detail, and of subsequent failure as a result of this oversight. Your energy level will be high and you want to get on with things, but you might move a little too fast. You could also overreach yourself in other ways, tiring yourself out or giving yourself high blood pressure as a result of all the extra stress you put on yourself. If you want to get in shape or take up a new sport, you will have the energy and motivation to do so. This is also a good time for travel and speculative ventures, and you can take the occasional gamble now.

Health problems might affect your liver or gall bladder, so try to avoid eating fatty foods, or eating too late at night.

Those with personal Year Numbers of 2,5,6,7 or 8 should try to avoid being too impulsive or bumptious.

House four

    Element: Wood
    Season: Late spring   2023
    Direction: Southeast

This is a time of rapid growth and advancement. The rural image is one of crops growing at a furious pace and animals feeding and becoming fat and healthy. This is a time of better weather, although still a little cool and wet at times, and the feeling is one of optimism. The sun rises higher in the eastern sky and the warm air drives up from the south (in the Northern Hemisphere, of course).

In personal terms, this is the time to go after whatever it is that you want, and pregnancy might be on your agenda. There is a kind of momentum that pushes all your enterprises towards the goal of success. Whether your mind is fixed upon business, financial matters, personal relationships, domestic matters or anything else that you want, a little effort now will pay off very quickly. This is the time to market yourself or to market any goods or services that you have to offer, because your ability to communicate to others will be especially effective now. This is the time to make yourself over and to brush up your social skills, so that you can be more attractive to others. If a better job or a promotion is in the air, you must do your best to be noticed in just the right way. In business, you must go after contracts or opportunities and be ready to expand. It should be easy for you to raise a loan at this time, if you need one. Advertising, judicious use of the media and putting the word around will be invaluable now, as would any kind of public speaking that serves the purpose of getting your name around. Communicating and liaising with important people is also part of the scene. However, in all these things you must guard against overdoing things, in order to avoid running out of money, strength or steam. If you fail at all during this phase, it will be entirely due to a lack of courage, a negative attitude or some other self-induced problem.

Health problems are likely to arise from overdoing things, so take time out to rest and play games, take a little exercise and relax your mind and body. Respiratory or stomach ailments are possible, as are colds and flu that result from getting cold and wet. Take a few hours or even a few days here and there to retreat, reflect and to go over things in your mind. This will stop your hell-for-leather rush to success long enough for you to take the time to spot anything you have missed, or something that might land you in trouble later on.

Those with personal Year Numbers of 2,5,6,7 or 8 should take care to rest and not to overdo things during this phase.

House five

Element:	Earth
Season:	The end of any season and the start of the next
Direction:	Center

The image here is of the changeover from one season to the next; the rural image could be one of starting to plough, watching the grapes in a winery and hoping the weather won't suddenly turn bad, or celebrating after gathering in the harvest and thinking about the next one. A Chinese compass doesn't only show the cardinal angles of north, south, east and west, but also the center. After each journey away, one returns to the center, and this phase represents returning, reassessing and preparing for the next phase.

In personal terms, this is a time of fluctuation and transition, which can feel like a belated adolescence. Now is the time to look back over what you have done so far, to measure your progress and also to look forward to the future with all its possibilities and uncertainties. There may be too many options open to you and you could be faced with a number of choices. Alternatively, you may have too much going on in your life, so that you are worn out much of the time and unable to do justice to any part of it.

There may be a Karmic reckoning to be faced now, or Karmic benefits to be reaped. Perhaps one side of your life is taking too much precedence while other aspects are being neglected, so balance is the thing to aim for. You will also need to strike a balance between what you do for others and what you do for yourself. You may need to search for a middle road between the demands of your family life, your job and time for yourself.

This is not likely to be a year of major change, but you will be in the center of everything that is going on around you, and there are times when you will feel as though you are in the eye of the hurricane. Having said this, you may be tempted to start new projects or to make important journeys, but the advice is to think deeply before doing any of these things. Holiday travel is fine, but anything more ambitious might be best left for another time. You may wish to look back to bad times in the past and perhaps speak out about hurts that you received, or you may wish to apologize to those whom you have hurt. Despite feeling an urge to push forward with your plans, your situation is so unpredictable that it is hard to say whether you would succeed or not. Basically, the message here is to tread water and to keep as calm as you can at this time, because nothing can really be relied upon.

Despite your determination to keep on a steady course, things might change of their own volition, and in this case you will have to strive for balance amid changing circumstances. You may have to deal with a great deal of upheaval and confrontation, but on a more positive note, you may find new ways of handling old situations.

The strong emphasis on the center as represented by the Element of Earth means that your home or premises could become a center of activities that might involve you in working from home, or in living in some kind of social center. Alternatively, you may set up a center of some kind. You won't have to travel far, because the world will find its way to you - possibly via the Internet. One feature of this period is that it can indicate changes in relationships so if you are lonely at the start of this period, things might well have changed by the end of it.

Serious health issues may arise, especially if these have been building up for some time. Expect a visit to the dentist this year, and don't take any health matter lightly. You may suffer from emotional ups and downs, partly in response to the things that are going on around you.

Those whose personal Year Number is 1,3 or 4 will feel the most uncomfortable during this period.

House six

Element: Metal
Season: Early autumn
Direction: Northwest

This is a time of high achievement and success. The rural image is of the start of the harvest whilst watching the remaining crops swell and ripen. The wind is turning slightly to the north and there are a few cooler days mingled with the hot ones.

In a personal sense, this is a time of prosperity and achievement, and even if this is not quite here yet, it soon will be. This is a good time in which to take charge of your life, and especially your business affairs. Business travel will be a success, and even if you don't travel, you will feel pleased with your efforts and your superiors will think well of you. The danger here is to become arrogant or boastful, or to believe that things will always be this good. The element of Metal always suggests determination and a disinclination to listen to what others have to say. If your situation is comfortable, happy and successful, you may be so pleased with yourself that you become convinced that your ideas are the only ones worth listening to, and that others have nothing useful to offer. This may work for a while, but it could put the first few nails in the coffin of relationships at work or in your personal life.

You will feel fit and strong, and as a result you may take on too much, or rush at jobs too quickly and without sufficient preparation, which could lead to accidents. Care must be taken when handling machinery or travelling, and any injuries must be treated immediately. You may try to force your opinions on others and you may become too dogmatic and demanding in your relationships with others. Take care not to pick fights, either at work or at home. Try to enjoy this period of success and prosperity without letting it go to your head.

Health problems might come from injuries, especially to the head.

House seven

Element:	Metal
Season:	Autumn
Direction:	West

The rural image is of the revelry that follows a harvest. The barn is full and the stock is doing well, market prices are good and there is milk, honey and a glass of cider all round. Everything you have done in the past has now paid off, and you can afford to rest and to take a holiday. This is the time to spend some money on your home and garden, and to treat your friends and loved ones to something special. Avoid spending everything you have, or living on credit, or you will find yourself short when the wind begins to blow in the other direction once again.

Your sex drive will be high, and whether this turns out to be a good or a bad thing depends upon your personal circumstances and your natural tendencies. If you are happily settled with someone, this is good news, but you could fall in love with someone who is bad for you, or fall into the trap of becoming obsessed. You could end up hurting others as a result of following up on a stupid attraction.

Health matters arise through dental and bone problems, accidents and colds that turn to bronchitis, also damage to the large intestine.

If your personal Year Number is 3,4 or 9, take special care not to become boastful, to alienate others or to take your loved ones for granted, because you will need their support when life becomes difficult once again.

House eight

Element:	Earth
Season:	Early winter
Direction:	Southeast

This is a time of extremes, because either nothing will happen, or everything will happen, or your life may fluctuate between these two points while this House number is in operation. There is no special rural image, except perhaps for a quiet time when little is happening, interspersed with sudden storms that send the farmer out to check on his stock or his crops.

This House is called stillness by the Chinese, and it reflects the stagnant feeling that may come over you at times during this period, but there will also be times when you are in the middle of great turmoil and unable to get much done. One image that fits this

House would be the aftereffects of a change of address, when one sits in the middle of a great deal of muddle with little time or money to spend on putting things right.

You may feel stagnant or impotent in some way, and periods of frustration are bound to occur. You may find yourself living or working among strangers, or you may push others away from you. It seems as though your normal points of reference are out of kilter. Nothing will ride along smoothly, because total stagnation is followed by everything happening at once, and vice versa. The greatest problems come from misunderstandings, so be clear about what you mean, and avoid dealing with those who can't or won't understand what it is that you want, or where it is that you are coming from.

Health issues might involve the circulatory system or bone and joint problems. You could be the victim of violence, due to others finding you uncommunicative and unresponsive.

If your personal Year Number is 1,3 or 4, you will become particularly frustrated during this phase.

House nine

Element: Fire

Season: Summer

Direction: South

The ancient Chinese loved the summer when the crops and animals were doing well and they and their families were healthy and happy. To them, this period represented a time of achievement. On a more personal note, this House position represents fame and fortune, a time of acclaim, success and achievement of ambitions. If you want to take full advantage of this period, go all out for success and ensure that your name is the one that is put forward. This is a time of optimism and expansion, and you should take every opportunity for advancement that comes your way, because you can put your message across successfully now. Even if you don't have a career or a job as such, you can make personal achievements and become a star within your own circle. Whatever your personal ambitions are, you can achieve them now and receive the recognition and acclaim that you deserve. Anything you want to achieve should be within your sights now.

The only drawback is that you might overreach yourself in some way and wear yourself out. You will irritate others if you become obstinate or boastful. Your increasingly public image means that you will have to behave very well, and if there are any skeletons in your cupboard, this is the time when they will emerge.

There is no reason to suspect that you would be ill during this time, but you should try to balance your work and social life with a little rest and some gentle exercise. There may be many calls upon you to be here, there and everywhere, and you must learn to turn some of these jobs down in order to preserve your strength. The fire element of the year could bring sudden fevers, burns, accidents, eye problems and heart or circulation problems. Take care when dealing with tools or machinery, or when cooking or dealing with hot things of any kind.

If your personal Year Number is 1,6 or 7, you may not be as happy or healthy as you ought to be during this phase.

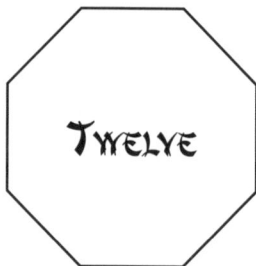

TWELVE

Weighing the Bones

Hour of birth - technique - tables for year, month, day & hour of birth - examples - interpreting the bone weights

Now for something really different! The background to Bone Weighing is obscure, but it comes from the same organization of the elements that is used in the more advanced forms of Chinese astrology. The Chinese use the word "bones" or skeleton in the same way that we would use the word "Roots" or foundations. Therefore, the bones in question could be called the roots of the system, so "weighing the bones" would be like going back to the origin of Chinese astrology. Having said this, Bone Weighing doesn't look at all like Chinese astrology, and it is altogether a much simpler form of divination.

The technique is easy to use and the readings that follow it could be classified as quaint, but the system does seem to work. However, as with any other divinatory system, you should make up your own mind whether or not you place any credence on the outcome.

This method of fortune telling doesn't require you to get on the scales in order to weigh your bones, because you only need to use the simple tables given below to discover your "bone" weight.

Hour of birth

About the only drawback to this system is that the hour of birth is used. Like many other Chinese systems, the day is broken into two hour blocks, so this gives quite a bit of leeway in cases where the exact time is not known. The system uses local time at the place of birth, but it is debatable whether one should deduct an hour for British Summer Time (BST) or for Daylight Saving. If you were born during the summer, I suggest that you ought to try deducting an hour and compare the two readings.

According to tradition, the heavier your bones, the luckier you will be, with a stable marriage, wealth, health and a straightforward, predictable kind of life. However, thin or light boned people have more interesting if less stable lives, while the lightest bones of all appear to have a dreadful time with no luck at all. This kind of "Karmic" viewpoint may well have been accurate in the bad old days, when people had no way of improving their lives; nowadays, of course, we have modern psychology, counselling and therapy, medical and many other advances that can help "lighter-boned" people.

The heaviest bones of all would occur for those born on the 18th, 26th of April, the 18th, 26th of October 1918, or the same dates during 1978, at a time of 9am to 11am, or 11pm to midnight. I will show you how this works out in the example section a little later in this chapter.

Technique

1. Consult the tables to find the weight of your bones for your year, month, day and hour of birth. The weights are given in ounces and decimals of ounces. This may sound tricky, but the system is actually very easy.

2. Add the weights of your bones for your year, month, day and hour of birth together, to discover their total weight.

3. Once you have found your weight, look up the reading.

Please note:

This table begins at 1924 and ends at 1983. For births before 1924, add 60 years. For births after 1983, deduct 60 years.
This gives you a figure that is within the "sleeve" of the table.

Example one: 1910 + 60 = 1970
Example two: 1989 - 60 = 1929

Table of weights for the year of birth

1924	1.2
1925	0.9
1926	0.6
1927	0.7
1928	1.2
1929	0.5
1930	0.9
1931	0.7
1932	0.7
1933	0.8
1934	1.5
1935	0.9
1936	1.6
1937	0.8
1938	0.8
1939	1.0
1940	1.2
1941	0.6
1942	0.8
1943	0.7
1944	0.5
1945	1.5
1946	0.6
1947	1.6
1948	1.5
1949	0.8

1950	0.9
1951	1.2
1952	1.0
1953	0.7
1954	1.5
1955	0.6
1956	0.5
1957	1.4
1958	1.4
1959	0.9
1960	0.7
1961	0.7
1962	0.9
1963	1.2
1964	0.8
1965	0.7
1966	1.3
1967	0.5
1968	1.4
1969	0.5
1970	0.9
1971	1.7
1972	0.5
1973	0.7
1974	1.2
1975	0.8
1976	0.8
1977	0.6
1978	1.9
1979	0.6
1980	0.8
1981	1.6
1982	1.0
1983	0.7

Table of weights for the month of birth

Jan	0.5
Feb	0.6
Mar	0.7
Apr	1.8
May	0.9
Jun	0.5
Jul	0.6
Aug	0.9
Sep	1.5
Oct	1.8
Nov	0.8
Dec	0.9

Table of weights for the day of birth

1	0.5
2	1.0
3	0.8
4	1.5
5	1.6
6	1.5
7	0.8
8	1.6
9	0.8
10	1.6
11	0.9
12	1.6
13	0.8
14	1.7
15	1.0
16	0.8
17	0.9
18	1.8
19	0.5
20	1.5

21	1.0
22	0.9
23	0.8
24	0.9
25	1.5
26	1.8
27	0.7
28	0.8
29	1.6
30	0.6
31	0.5

Table of weights for the hour of birth

11pm to 1am	1.6
1am to 3am	0.6
3am to 5am	0.7
5am to 7am	1.0
7am to 9am	0.9
9am to 11am	1.6
11am to 1pm	1.0
1pm to 3pm	0.8
3pm to 5pm	0.8
5pm to 7pm	0.8
7pm to 9pm	0.6
9pm to 11pm	0.6

Example

The example that I have used here is for my friend, Helen. She was born during the summer, but because her time of birth comes within the same two-hour band, with or without deducting an hour for British Summer Time, the weight remains the same for either hour.

Helen

Year:	1965	0.7
Month:	August	0.9
Day:	21st	1.0
Hour:	2.18am BST	0.6
	(1.18am GMT)	
TOTAL:		3.2

Here is another example this time for another friend, Sandy. Sandy was also born during the summer, but his hour bone weight again remains the same, with or without deducting an hour for BST.

Sandy

Year:	1968	1.4
Month:	July	1.6
Day:	31st	0.5
Hour:	8.35pm BST	0.6
	(7.35pm GMT)	
TOTAL:		4.1

According to the list, both of these examples will have unstable but interesting lives with much travel, changes of career and possible changes of marriage partner. Let us hope that they are happy with their interesting lives - whatever happens.

Now at last, for the example of the heaviest bones of all:

Example

Year (1918 or 1978):	1.9
Month (April or October):	1.8
Day (18th or 26th):	1.6
Hour (9am to 11am or 11pm to midnight):	1.6
TOTAL:	7.1

Interpreting bone weights

2.2   Dreadful; a life of penury, coldness and struggling to make a living.

2.3   Drifting, abandonment, wandering and never finding a permanent home.

2.4   Nobody will love you, there will be nothing to achieve, a wasted life.

2.5   Exile, being excluded from a family, but things may look up later in life.

2.6   You start out alone and poor, but things improve later on.

2.7   Hard work with little help from others, but you can make it if you try.

2.8   You may be too unrealistic to make a success of your life.

2.9   The first half of your life is awful, but by middle age things improve greatly.

3.0   A life of hard work and much travel.

3.1   You work hard when young and reap rewards when you are older.

3.2   You start out in a small way, but success builds slowly.

3.3   Travel and little success when young, but happiness and prosperity when old.

3.4   Yours is a religious or spiritual outlook.

3.5   Caution should be your watchword, as you are likely to be swindled.

3.6   If you work hard, nothing bad will come your way.

3.7   Many ups and downs, money comes and goes.

3.8   Weak health and bad luck in youth, but 30 brings a turning point for the better.

3.9   It is hard for you to make a success of anything.

4.0   A tough, single-minded attitude pays dividends in the end.

4.1   You are a rebel when young, but more conservative later in life.

4.2   Life may be quite dull at first, but money and fame come later on.

4.3   You are soft hearted and a bit of a loser, but you learn much and gain money later.

4.4   Take life easy and don't kill yourself working, because success will come.

4.5   Peace is hard to find, but with support you can fulfil your hopes.

4.6   Much travel and change; settle in a warm place if you can.

4.7   A good life with many good children, money flows in.

4.8   Work hard while young in order to reap the rewards later on.

4.9   Friends will help you to build for the future. Success later.

5.0   A self-centered attitude when young, an improved attitude brings success later.

5.1   It takes a while for you to find the right way, then happiness and success comes.

5.2   Luck and an easy life.

5.3   You will always have money.

5.4   Plenty to eat, a good home, great clothes, as long as you are honest and hard working.

5.5   A slow start, then fortune smiles.

5.6   Intellectual and wise, you never stop learning. Much travel and many experiences.

5.7   A happy, easy life with good fortune.

5.8   Fame, fortune and a long life.

5.9   You will go far, travel and do well in life.

6.0   Education brings opportunities, wealth, honor, land and property.

6.1   Wealth, fame and honor.

6.2   Education, wisdom and intellect will take you far.

6.3   You will achieve something special and earn a place in history.

6.4   You will reach a position of authority and make lots of money.

6.5   A military life would bring honors. If you choose some other lifestyle, you can fight your way to the top.

6.6   A life filled with beauty, wealth, fortune.

6.7   You come from a good family, money surrounds you and it always will.

6.8   An up and down life with great success after a few wilderness years.

6.9   Wealth, fame, honor and pleasure will be your destiny.

7.0   You will reach the highest strata of society with wealth, fame and success.

7.1   Wealth, power, success and honors.

THIRTEEN

The Chien Tung: Yarrow Stick Divination

What are yarrow sticks? - yarrow sticks & the I Ching - yarrow sticks & the Tarot - I Ching stones

What are Yarrow sticks?

Yarrow is a plant that is also known as milfoil or by its formal name, achillea millefolium. It has particularly straight stalks, which means that they can be sliced by hand into nice straight sticks. When the stalks have been cut and dried out, they are sliced and cut to length. The Chinese keep their yarrow sticks wrapped in a silk cloth and placed inside a box or a vase-like container with a lid, which is kept on a special shelf or a kind of wall-mounted alter, above the height of a man's shoulder. When the sticks are unwrapped for use, they are placed on a cloth in order to keep them away from any surface that might have been used for mundane purposes. Like our modern day Tarot cards, yarrow sticks are treated with reverence.

You may be able to find imitation Yarrow sticks in a Chinatown shop. These are usually sold in a black and red wooden container, and each stick is conveniently numbered in both English and Chinese. If you can't find commercial sticks, you can make them out of firelighter "spills" by choosing the straightest ones and writing numbers on them. Traditionally speaking, there should be 78 yarrow sticks, but if you make enough to create a nice bundle of a couple of dozen sticks, the system will work perfectly well.

Yarrow sticks and the I Ching

Ancient sources of Chinese information tell us that Yang numbers are odd while Yin numbers are even, so when you shake the container and extract the stick that first emerges from it, you must note whether the number on it is odd or even. If odd, write down a straight I Ching line; if even, note down a broken I Ching line.

Shake the container again and again, extracting sticks until you have six lines, building them upwards from the bottom line; this will give you your six lines of an I Ching hexagram. After this, it is a simple matter of reading through the I Ching section of this book for an interpretation.

There is another really ancient method of selection called "dividing the Yarrow sticks", that involves putting a certain number of sticks between certain fingers in a certain order. The method is so desperately complex that I decided not to reproduce it here.

Yarrow sticks and the Tarot

I found a proper set of Yarrow sticks when visiting Hong Kong, but the typical booklet that accompanied them gave the silliest readings imaginable. Fortunately, as there happen to be 78 sticks and by coincidence there are also 78 Tarot cards, it is an easy matter to adapt the sticks for use with the Tarot. I have tried to keep this book strictly Chinese and the Tarot is not known as a Chinese divination, but some scholars suggest that the origins of the Tarot were once Chinese, so I think I can be forgiven for including it.

For the purposes of this book, I have taken the ancient Tarot idea of arranging the four suits of the Minor Arcana according to their seasons, with Wands for spring, Cups for summer, Pentacles for autumn and Swords for winter. This seasonal idea is a very Chinese concept, so it fits very well with the atmosphere of this book.

Tarot correlation

0. The Fool (number 0
   or number 78)
1. The Magician
2. The High Priestess
3. The Empress
4. The Emperor
5. The Hierophant
6. The Lovers
7. The Chariot
8. Strength
9. The Hermit
10. The Wheel of Fortune
11. Justice
12. The Hanged Man
13. Death
14. Temperance
15. The Devil
16. The Tower
17. The Star
18. The Moon
19. The Sun
20. Judgement
21. The World
22. Ace of wands
23. Two of wands
24. Three of wands
25. Four of wands
26. Five of wands
27. Six of wands
28. Seven of wands
29. Eight of wands
30. Nine of wands
31. Ten of wands

32. Page of wands
33. Knight of wands
34. Queen of wands
35. King of wands
36. Ace of cups
37. Two of cups
38. Three of cups
39. Four of cups
40. Five of cups
41. Six of cups
42. Seven of cups
43. Eight of cups
44. Nine of cups
45. Ten of cups
46. Page of cups
47. Knight of cups
48. Queen of cups
49. King of cups
50. Ace of pentacles
51. Two of pentacles
52. Three of pentacles
53. Four of pentacles
54. Five of pentacles
55. Six of pentacles
56. Seven of pentacles
57. Eight of pentacles
58. Nine of pentacles
59. Ten of pentacles
60. Page of pentacles
61. Knight of pentacles
62. Queen of pentacles
63. King of pentacles
64. Ace of swords

65. Two of swords
66. Three of swords
67. Four of swords
68. Five of swords
69. Six of swords
70. Seven of swords
71. Eight of swords
72. Nine of swords
73. Ten of swords
74. Page of swords
75. Knight of swords
76. Queen of swords
77. King of swords
78. The Fool (number 78 or number 0)

I Ching Stones

Here is yet another really ancient and rather nice variation in the tools you can use to create an I Ching reading.

If you enjoy making your own divination tools, you can make a set of I Ching stones. You will need to find six flat stones and then paint broken lines on three of them and unbroken lines on the other three.

Place all the stones in a bag and shake them up. Without looking, reach into the bag, take out one stone and put it onto a clean table, preferably covered with a pretty cloth. Take out the next stone, put it above the first and keep repeating this until you have all six stones in a line, with the last one you pick up being at the top. This will give you an I Ching hexagram.

An alternative method of preparing your hexagram, which also gives you the changing lines, is to pick three stones out of the bag and then see whether you have a majority of unbroken Yang lines, or a majority of broken Yin lines. If you pick a majority of

Yang lines, draw an unbroken Yang line on a piece of paper. If you pick a majority of (broken) Yin lines, draw a broken Yin line on the paper. Put the stones back in the bag, shake it and repeat the process, drawing your second line above the first. Continue doing this until you have six lines. Any lines that arise from three stones all with the same Yang or Yin line upon them become "changing lines". The chapter on the I Ching will show you what to do about "changing lines", although for an in-depth explanation of the readings derived from "changing lines", you will need a book dedicated to the I Ching alone.

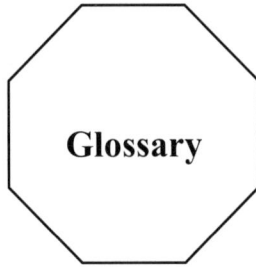

Glossary

Active year
A term for a Yang year in Chinese astrology. Otherwise, active stands for the positive, masculine Yang force.

Animal signs
The twelve Chinese zodiac animals (Rat, Ox, etc.). These can rule a year, a month or an hour.

Binary system
Used in computing, which may have been originally inspired by the I Ching.

Binomials
The elements of Wood, Fire etc. in Chinese astrology.

Chi
Also spelled Ki or Qui. Basically, vibrations, energies or a wind that blows in the right direction for good fortune, and the wrong one for bad fortune.

Chinese almanac
A Chinese form of ephemeris or book of tables for working out Chinese astrology and the Four Pillars.

Coins
Usually Chinese fortune telling coins used in the I Ching, but any coins will do.

Earthly branches
The animal zodiac as used in Chinese astrology. Also doubles up in the Four Pillars and other systems.

Elements
The five elements of Wood, Fire, Earth, Metal and Water rule consecutive two year blocks (and much else) in Chinese astrology. They

are also incorporated into many other divinations, such as Feng Shui etc.

Feng Shui

A way of organizing a place in order to bring good fortune.

Fortune cookies

Delicious, and fun too!

Four Emperors

Another name for the Four Pillars of Destiny.

Four Pillars of Destiny

A Chinese horoscope chart system that gives full character readings and which can also be used for prediction.

Heaven

Apart from the obvious, this is a term used to describe the upper part of the face in face reading. It also applies to one of the trigrams of the I Ching.

Heavenly stems

The elements used in Chinese astrology and the I Ching.

Hexagrams

64 sets of broken and unbroken lines grouped in sixes; part of the I Ching.

I Ching

A system of broken and unbroken lines that are grouped together into sets for fortune telling.

Key Magic Square

The basic Magic Square that is used in the Lo Shu for divination and in Feng Shui for beneficial directions and placements.

Lo Shu

Also known as the Nine Star Ki. A numerological system that is widely used in China for divination.

Lunar oracle

A set predictive reading for every day of the month, starting with a new moon.

Magic Square

Used for divination in the Lo Shu system and for fortunate directions and placements in Feng Shui.

Mah Jong
A game that is extremely popular in China and was also popular in the UK in the 1920s. The Mah Jong pieces can be used for fortune telling in much the same way as runes or Tarot cards.

Ming Shu
Chinese astrology.

Pa Kua
The eight-sided symbol, often with a mirror in the middle, which is taken from the I Ching and used in Feng Shui.

Receptive
A term for a Yin year in Chinese astrology. It has feminine connotations.

Seasons
Spring, summer, autumn, winter. Spring either starts with the Chinese New Year in any year, or it can be set from February 4.

Sticks
Chinese fortune telling sticks.

Stones
Chinese fortune telling stones.

Tarot
The western familiar form of divination cards.

Trigrams
Sets of three broken and unbroken lines that are grouped together, which form the basis of the I Ching and much else besides.

Weighing bones
A numerology system.

Yang
The positive, masculine force.

Yarrow sticks
Chinese fortune telling sticks.

Yin
The receptive, feminine force.

CROSS REFERENCES

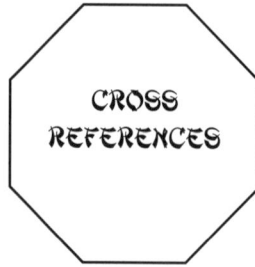

Cross References and Background

Many of the systems in this book use the same root concepts of the elements, the family group and the Lo Shu. Chinese people and those who are influenced by Chinese thinking grow up with these ideas in the same way that westerners are familiar with Bible stories, or Hindu people are familiar with the myths and legends of their Gods. This makes Chinese divination easy for Oriental people to grasp, but it makes it extremely difficult for those of us in the west who are not switched on to the archetypes. This cross-reference section is designed to help you understand some of the background to many of the divinations in this book.

Yang

The masculine and positive force of energy, drive, effectiveness, action, sex, construction, battle, self-defense, speed. Without some machismo and testosterone there would be no progress. Yang is the locomotive of history, albeit sometimes excessively, through engineering ald also war and destruction.

Yin

The feminine and negative principle of endurance, patience, nurturing, conserving, protecting, caring, feeding, waiting, caution, immobility. Without this estrogen force, everything would fall apart and the world would come to an end. By the same token, too much Yin can hinder progress.

The trigrams of the I Ching
These are some of the oldest archetypes in the world; they go back at least 5,000 years and vie with the gods of ancient Egypt for longevity.

Ch'ien (trigram here)
Fully Yang.
Father.
Heaven.
Strength, power, action, firmness, creativity, strength, logic.
Associated with the full force of masculine authority and power.
The south. To astrologers living in the Northern Hemisphere, the sun and mid-heaven were always towards the south. The sun is considered to be life giving, but too much heat and drought is dangerous to crops, animals and humans alike.
The element of Fire, the color red and the Phoenix are associated with the Father and the south.

Tui (trigram)
Lake.
Youngest daughter.
Joy, pleasure, over-indulgence, sensual pleasure and satisfaction, tenderness.
Associated with the sweetness of a young girl, but also with that of a young lover.

Li (trigram)
Strongly Yang.
Fire.
Eldest son.
In some traditions, also the middle daughter.
Intelligence, loyalty, beauty, elegance.
Associated with love, intelligence, expertise and loyalty.
East. The direction of sunrise, which is associated with springtime, optimism and good fortune. The element of Wood and the color green are associated with the Eldest Son and the east.
The animal is the Dragon.

Chen (trigram)
Thunder.
Middle son.
Energy, violence, thunder, shocks, awakening.
Like the Tower in the Tarot, this brings shocks, possible havoc and disaster, but also awakenings and enlightenment.

Sun (trigram)
Wind.
Eldest daughter.
Gentleness, patience, persistence, justice, progress, sometimes dissolution.
A reliable and comforting image that rights the wrongs of life.

K'an (trigram)
Strongly Yin.
Water.
Middle son.
In some traditions, the middle daughter.
Danger, difficulty, but also lack of fear. Instinct and intuition.
Water finds its own level, and this shows that ways out of difficulty can be found.
The west. This is the direction of the sunset and it is associated with autumn. The ideas are a mixture of relief and joy that the harvest can be gathered in, but also fear of the approach of winter. Metal tools can now be cleaned, mended and put away for the winter.
The element is Metal and the color white, which is the color of death and mourning.
The animal associated with the Middle Son and the west is the Tiger.

Ken (trigram)
Mountain.
Youngest son.
Quiet, calm, repose, stasis, stillness, withdrawal, meditation.
This represents retreat, reflection, a time to withdraw from action, to rest and meditate.

K'un

Fully Yin.

The earth (this is the actual earth rather than the element of Earth)

Mother.

Passive, receptive, acquiescent, patient, dedicated, fertile.

Clearly the opposite of the first trigram, which is the Father; this is an image of pure womanhood and motherhood.

North. The season of winter in northern China is not liked, because of the extreme cold and also heavy rain, floods, ice and snow and darkness. Nevertheless, it is valued as being a quiet period in rural life when tools can be mended and farm buildings fixed up.

The element is Water and the traditional color of this direction is black, but dark blue and dark brown are also associated with this direction.

The animal associated with the Mother and the north is the long-lived Tortoise, or sometimes the Turtle.

The heavenly stems

The heavenly stems are the Elements in Chinese astrology; they link to the trigrams as described above and to most other divinations as well. The elements are usually expressed in the order of Wood, Fire, Earth, Metal and Water, which is considered to be the creative cycle.

Wood creates Fire. Fire creates Earth (ashes). Earth creates Metal. Metal can flow like Water. Water irrigates Wood. The cycle is poor when an element is juxtaposed against another that is two away from itself; this is considered to be incompatible or destructive. Thus Wood and Earth are incompatible.

In Chinese astrology, the elements form a ten-year cycle with each element ruling consecutive two-year periods. These are known as the binomials because two years use the same name. The year 2000 is a Metal Dragon year, while the year 2001 is a Metal Snake year, so these belong to the Metal binomial.

The earthly branches

Since Buddhist times, these have become the familiar Chinese zodiac animals of Rat, Ox, Tiger, Rabbit, Dragon, Snake, Horse, Goat,

Rooster, Dog and Pig. The Rat is Yang, the Ox is Yin, the Tiger is Yang and so on, alternating through the system.

Before the Buddhists popularized these animals, the earthly branches were a repeat of the elements, but used in a monthly cycle rather than the annual one. This was also attached to the annual cycle in a confusing and complicated manner. You will see more about this in the chapters on Chinese astrology and the Four Pillars of Destiny.

The Pa Kua and Feng Shui

The Pa Kua is that famous eight-sided symbol with the eight trigrams placed around it. In this case, each trigram represents a direction that is used to select the right direction to travel in or to build a house or a business in. You will find out about this in the Feng Shui section of this book.

There seem to be variations in the way the directions link to the original trigrams, and some of the corresponding ideas contradict each other. I have seen writers of some books get themselves into a dreadful muddle when trying to link the directions and seasons to each other.

The Feng Shui and Lo Shu sections of this book are probably best treated as stand-alone systems that borrow from other ideas, such as the I Ching or astrology, without linking with them too precisely.

READING LIST

Further Reading List

I gained much of my knowledge of Chinese divinations through traveling and talking with others who use these systems, and also by using them myself over a period of time.

I have double-checked some of my ideas and experiences in some of the books in this list. Others were of no use to me for this particular project, but they are of interest to anyone who is keen to study more about Chinese divination.

TAO TE CHING
Lao Tzu
Wordsworth Editions Limited, 1997
THE CHINESE PAKUA
Ong Hean-Tatt
Pelanduk Publications, 1991
I CHING
Chris Marshall
Simon & Schuster Inc., 1962
I CHING
Sam Reifler
Bantam, 1974
THE COMPLETE I CHING
Edward Albertson
Sherbourne Press Inc., 1969
I CHING, THE No. 1 SUCCESS FORMULA
Christopher Markert

Aquarian, 1986
THE VISUAL I CHING
Oliver Perrottet
Michael Joseph, 1987
I CHING COIN PREDICTION
Da Liu, 1975
THE I CHING WORKBOOK
R L Wing
Doubleday, 1979
THE HANDBOOK OF CHINESE HOROSCOPES
Theodora Lau
HarperCollins, 1979
CHINESE ASTROLOGY
Man-Ho Kwok
Cassell plc, 1998
CHINESE ANIMAL SYMBOLS
Ong Hean-Tatt
Pelanduk Publications, 1993
NINE STAR KI
Robert Sachs
Element 1992
**THE WAY TO CHINESE ASTROLOGY;
THE FOUR PILLARS OF DESTINY**
Jean-Michel Huon de Kermadec
Unwin Paperbacks, 1983
CHINESE FACE AND HAND READING
Man-Ho Kwok
Piatkus, 1999
FACE FORTUNES
Peter Shen
Pelanduk Publications, 1997
(A particularly good book on the subject)
DR YIN NU'S FACE READING DECODER
Dynamo House Pty. Ltd.

CHINESE ALMANAC
Ting Tai Book Company
THE JAPANESE FORTUNE CALENDAR
Robert Chiba
Charles E. Tuttle Company Inc, 1965
CHINESE FORTUNE READING
Peter Shen
Pelanduk Publications, 1998
TAOIST ASTROLOGY
Susan Levitt and Jean Tang
Destiny Books, 1997
THE CHINESE HOROSCOPES GUIDE TO
RELATIONSHIPS
Theodora Lau
Doubleday, 1997
FENG SHUI
Jonathan Dee
Caxton Editions, 1999
FENG SHUI FOR BEGINNERS
Richard Craze
Hodder & Stoughton, 1994
FENG SHUI LOVE
Lillian Too
Element Books, 1997
FENG SHUI WEALTH
Lillian Too
Element Books, 1997
FENG SHUI HEALTH
Lillian Too
Element Books, 1997
FENG SHUI
Jon Sandifer
Piatkus, 1999
FENG SHUI ASTROLOGY
Jon Sandifer

240   Chinese Divinations

Piatkus, 1997
(A very clear guide to complicated concepts)
THE WAY OF FENG SHUI
Philippa Waring
Seventh Zenith Ltd, 1993
FENG SHUI FOR BUSINESS
Evelyn Lip
Times Editions Pte. Ltd., 1989
FENG SHUI FOR THE HOME
Evelyn Lip
Times Editions Pte. Ltd., 1986
FENG SHUI IN YOUR GARDEN
Roni Jay and Richard Craze
Thorsons, 1998
PRACTICAL FENG SHUI
Richard Craze
Lorenz Books, 1997
THE FENG SHUI HANDBOOK
Lam Kam Chuen
Gaia Books Ltd., 1995
THE PERSONAL FENG SHUI MANUAL
Lam Kam Chuen
Gaia Books Ltd., 1998
FENG SHUI & DESTINY FOR FAMILIES
Ramond Lo
Times Editions Pte. Ltd., 1999
FENG SHUI
Stephen Skinner
Parragon, 1997
LILLIAN TOO'S LITTLE BOOK OF FENG SHUI
Lillian Too
Element, 1998
**LILLIAN TOO'S LITTLE BOOK OF FENG SHUI
AT WORK**
Lillian Too

Element, 1999
COLLINS GEM FENG SHUI
Richard Craze
HarperCollins, 1999
EASTERN SYSTEMS FOR WESTERN ASTROLOGERS
Introduced by Thomas Moore
Samuel Weiser Inc., 1997
ANNUAL HOROSCOPE BOOKS
Edward Li Kui Ming
World center of Master Li Kui Ming's Feng Shui products and publications, Hong Kong.
ROCKY SUNG'S CHINESE ASTROLOGY AND FENG SHUI 2000
Rocky Sung
Thorsons, 1999
LEARN CHINESE CHARACTERS IN HONG KONG
Chan Kwok Kin and William Crewe
Greenwood Press, 1992
CHIEN TUNG - CHINESE FORTUNE STICKS
(I've no idea who wrote or printed this!)
THE KEW GARDENS TAKEAWAY MENU
(Yes, really!)

Index

V
Vega 6

W
Water hand 105
Weighing the Bones 214
Winds, The 158
Wood 42
Wood hand 105
Writers' Guild vi

Y
Yang and Yin 10, 94
Yang and Yin signs 10
Yarrow 224
Yarrow Stick Divination 224
Yarrow sticks and the Tarot 225
Year number 178
Year Numbers 178, 198

Z
Zones 70

Astrology... on the Move!

"Where on Earth should you be?"

Sasha's book shows how any geographic location exerts a major influence on your life, and how a change of location can affect you, by way of a long-term move, or even simply choosing the right venue to ensure an enjoyable vacation.

In her well-known, uncomplicated writing style, Sasha shows you how to use and understand three different mapping techniques. The first has become popular from the development of Jim Lewis's registered system of Astro*Carto*Graphy™. Secondly, the Local Space system devised by Michael Erlewine, and finally, the much older but stunningly effective system of Astro-Geodetics, worked on by Sasha herself in the early 1970s.

You don't have to be an astrologer to use and understand geographic astrology. Few other books exist on the subject; none are as accessible as this one.

"This book will help you to understand better where you have been, are now, and are going in the future."
Roy Gillett, President, Astrological Association of Great Britain

Paperback, ISBN 0-9533478-0-X
£9.99

Prophecy for Profit

"The essential Career & Business Guide for those who give Readings"

Sasha Fenton and her husband Jan Budkowski combine decades of divinatory & financial skills in this internationally oriented book.

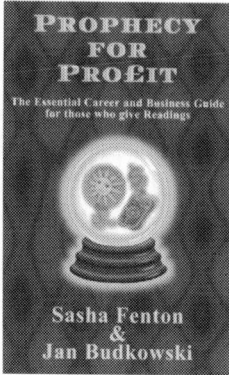

Subjects covered include:
Organisational methods... A mental & physical health guide... Starting-up costs... Building up your clientele... Managing finance & cashflow... Working in fairs & festivals... The Marine Bandsman Syndrome... Psychic protection... Teaching & Lecturing... and much more!

If you're serious about your career, this is the book for you - whatever your divination, from Astrology to Zoomancy!

"This book is a true gemstone. It should be on every Reader's MUST HAVE list, and should be recommended to anyone working part time or professionally, or indeed considering Reading as a vocation."
Andrew Smith, The Celtic Astrologer magazine

Paperback, ISBN 0-9533478-1-8   £10.95